Cheers for
Girls Only

"Wickedly funny and poignant . . . An utter delight, *Girls Only* is tea at the Stanhope in the raucous, irreverent, and ultimately delicious company of those who know you best and love you most."

—*BOOKPAGE*

"In *Girls Only*, Alex Witchel's beat is her own family. What a good reporter she is! Her book is sweet and tough-minded, funny and serious."

—SUSAN ISAACS

"Wickedly observant . . . Ms. Witchel is sardonic, mournful, and hilarious, sometimes all at once . . . In an era of mom-bashing, it's refreshing to read about a passionate mother-lover."

—*THE NEW YORK TIMES*

"My mother will wish Alex Witchel was her daughter. This loving, witty, and wise book is a tribute to life with Mother. It's not for girls only, it's for anyone who loves his or her family."

—WENDY WASSERSTEIN

Girls Only

✳

Sleepovers, Squabbles, Tuna Fish
and Other Facts of Family Life

ALEX WITCHEL

A Touchstone Book

Published by Simon & Schuster

New York   London   Toronto   Sydney

 Touchstone
A Division of Simon & Schuster, Inc.
1230 Avenue of the Americas
New York, NY 10020

First Touchstone trade paperback edition January 2008

TOUCHSTONE and colophon are registered trademarks of Simon & Schuster, Inc.

For information about special discounts for bulk purchases,
please contact Simon & Schuster Special Sales at 1-800-456-6798
or business@simonandschuster.com.

Designed by Mary Austin Speaker

Manufactured in the United States of America

10   9   8   7   6   5   4   3   2   1

Library of Congress Cataloging-in-Publication Data is available.

ISBN-13: 978-0-7432-5492-2
ISBN-10:   0-7432-5492-9

For Frank, Sam, Greg,
Emmett, Nat and Simon—
who stayed home.

Acknowledgments

I would like to thank first and foremost the editor of *Girls Only*, Peter Gethers, who's incredibly smart—for a boy; my agent, Kathy Robbins, who saw a book long before I did—and did something about it; John Montorio, my editor at *The New York Times*, who makes my life there worth living; June Havoc, for letting me use her life to examine my own; Barbara Denner, whose capacity for my kvetching is nothing short of heroic; Cynthia LaBorde, who works harder than anyone I know and is always my inspiration; Dr. Stephen J. Nicholas at Lenox Hill Hospital, whose expertise and great patience have brought high heels back into my life; Ben Cheever, whose shoulder is the most absorbent in town; my mom, Barbara Witchel, for letting me share her with the rest of the world; my sister, Phoebe Witchel, for letting me share my mom.

And most of all, my husband, Frank Rich, the true gift of my life.

Contents

Introduction

✻

I am the oldest child, and even though I have a sister and two brothers, I have always considered myself the only child.

Surprised? Don't be. There isn't an eldest child alive who doesn't secretly think the same thing, and though I can't speak from experience, I suspect the babies of the family feel the same way. It's those middle children who would object, but the poor things have no choice. They've got to do something to get attention.

My family has its own unique configuration, which goes like this:

First, there is me. First child, first grandchild, eyewitness to the tiny apartment before the first house—not to mention all those long-gone relatives the rest only know from home movies, the ones with the red lipstick and flabby upper arms, which never stopped them from wearing the latest in strapless taffeta.

Three years after me came Greg. I have promised to leave him out of this tale as much as possible since, as a classic middle child, his way of getting attention is to demand none.

But here's where it gets interesting. In a marked departure from her early sixties' peers, my mom decided, after she had two children, to renounce Donna Reed as a role model and earn her doctorate in educational psychology. So until I was ten the only intruder in my world was Greg. But, alas, my father, Sam, who works on Wall Street—though you could pay me a million dollars and I still couldn't explain what he does—always felt it was his personal mission to remedy the Holocaust by being fruitful and multiplying. So, when my mom finished her degree, she went back to work and back to babies.

Phoebe was next. I came home from the fourth grade for lunch one day and there she was in her brand-new crib. Bright red and screaming so hard that all the cords in her newborn neck stood out. And you know what? She wasn't making a sound. None at all. Which tells you everything you need to know about being a middle child, with the added indignity of being the second middle child.

Emmett came three years later, on New Year's Eve. I was thirteen by then and more concerned that the color of my choker match my bell-bottoms than about an occurrence as mundane as the arrival of a new baby had become in our house. The most attention I paid him was being the only one with the grace to faint dead away at his circumcision, which, quaintly enough, was held in our Scarsdale living room, right in front of the grandfather clock. I couldn't help but think of the prayer that Orthodox Jewish men say, in which they thank God they were not born women. Fools!

Anyway, now the lineup was even: two girls and my mom, two boys and my dad. One family of a girl and a boy, then a second one ten years later. But almost from the start, it seems, we broke on gender lines rather than age. The boys raked leaves, shoveled snow and threw softballs. They learned to talk about the stock market and where to gas up the car for less. The girls set the table, cleaned up and went shopping. We learned to talk about feelings and which department store had the best Clinique bonus. The only politically correct thing in our house was being a Democrat.

The boys meant business, in our family, and my father was the CEO:

What did you get on your report card?

How much is your allowance and why do you need more?

Who won the War of 1812?

But the girls meant home. They were the ones who asked:

How did you sleep?

What did you dream?

Can I borrow your pearls?

What I learned from my father was the boys' lesson of dealing in the world—trust no one and win the first time.

What I learned from my mother was the girls' lesson—trust no one and win the first time, but just in case you don't, come home, eat something, talk about it, have a drink, cry a little, then go back out there and try again.

What can I say? I enjoyed being a girl.

So that's how it happened, with no conscious decision on anyone's part, really, that as the years went by, my mom, my sister and I formed our own family within the family.

Girls Only.

Girls Only

*

chapter one

The Green Couch

O nce I was married, things changed.

I guess I should have known they would. Everyone says change is good and healthy and part of life, but I hate it. Even when it's for the better.

Don't get me wrong, I like being married. There are just fewer nights to hang out with Mom and Phoebe and stage our comfort marathons.

The day I got married, actually, was the last time we really were together. It was a Sunday, the ceremony wasn't until six, and they came to my apartment around noon. For my last meal, so to speak, I had requested Mom's tuna-fish casserole (heaven on earth) that she brought along with an armload of her potential outfits. This was because I was having a wedding that she didn't understand, meaning there was no aisle, no orchestra and no chopped liver.

What I had wanted instead of a hotel ballroom with a bandleader,

third cousins from Brooklyn and a Viennese table, was a grand total of
sixty people at Alison on Dominick Street, a small restaurant in SoHo,
where there would be a rabbi and frisée all in one room. I was not wearing
white (after years of using Mom's wedding dress to play fairy princesses
on Halloween, I couldn't take it seriously, so I chose an antique pink lace,
quite lovely, thank you) and the dress didn't even touch my ankles. Insur-
rection!

Which was why Mom had brought everything from ballgowns to
business suits with her in the hopes that before the wedding began she
might not only identify but even rationalize what this event was going to be. This was her particular form of schizophrenia at work: after
breaking enough barriers to brand herself a career woman in spite of
being a mother, she felt compelled to indulge these guilty retro lapses
where she had to conform or die. So, in the middle of writing her doc-
toral thesis, she would suddenly start baking pies from scratch. Then
she would be so exhausted and irritated at how much time she had spent
not doing her actual work that her mood would shift again and the
dining-room table would become invisible under piles of papers and
she wouldn't pick her head up for days.

This means that, in theory, if I had chosen a mountaintop in Tibet
for the wedding, she would, as a forward-thinking woman, applaud
my novelty, but when it came right down to the nuts and bolts of her
Bronx-born Jewish-mother checklist, I was nothing short of a disas-
ter—starting with my age, thirty-three, which she considered wizened
(*she* had been married at twenty-three), and ending with my insistence
on keeping my own name. She absolutely detested the notion that the
doorman or the butcher might not realize that I had indeed crossed the
finish line and become a bona fide Mrs.

So, on this day when the skies were as gray as my long-gone bunny
blanket, which everyone said I would walk down the aisle with because I
loved it so much, but couldn't because my beloved parents had dumped

it when I was twelve on the grounds of conduct unbecoming a preteen and I was *still* resenting it, I devoured containers of tuna-fish casserole, cold. I couldn't even wait the five minutes it would have taken to heat it up. I was starved, because I hadn't eaten all week, convinced I would look fat in my dress. But I knew I had to wise up now or I would faint dead away in the middle of the ceremony.

When I was finished, I managed to do my own hair and worry a pimple to death with seventeen layers of foundation. Somehow, the indignity of being an old maid breaking out on her wedding day was more than I could bear.

"Look at this!" I wailed to Mom.

"Where? I don't see anything," she said.

"Here, look, right next to my mouth. It's disgusting. I can't possibly be married with this on my face. He's going to take one look at me and leave."

"Alex, please, it's a little thing. You're the only one who knows it's there. You look stunning."

I watched her watch me. I was her daughter, it was my wedding day and she absolutely believed what she was saying. To her, I was always beautiful. And smart. Perfect. It occurred to me that I should marry her instead.

Phoebe was calm. Even though she has always wanted the kind of traditional wedding my mother was hoping, with three hours to go, that I still might have, she had no trouble adapting to my variation. Phoebe, ten years my junior, is a freethinking girl, as long as nothing gets in the way of what she wants for herself. I like Phoebe, actually. It's hard not to, since she loves me with all the genuine affection, admiration and abject terror any little sister has for one who's so much older. Like me and like Mom, she can be tough in the outside world, but she can also be warm, loyal and endlessly supportive even though we're completely different in so many ways. Including the physical. I am short, blonde and small. She is tall, dark and statuesque. This is a girl who's never shortened a sleeve in her life.

And even though she had not had a boyfriend in years, she was firmly committed to nuptials on the scale of Prince Charles and Lady Diana. What did she care that I chose an event of such modesty it wouldn't even qualify as her shower? She had bought a perfect dinner suit for the occasion, pink with black trim, and in her capacity as maid of honor and entire wedding party, was now fooling with the calla lilies I was going to carry in memory of Grandma, my mother's mother, who had carried them at her own wedding.

Mom started modeling her wardrobe. "How about this?" she asked brightly, trying on a skirt and blazer.

"Mom, it's a wedding, not a parent-teacher night," I said. "And don't even think about trying that," I added, pointing to a coral evening gown with a matching chiffon scarf. "May I point out that it is already three in the afternoon and you still don't know what to wear? Why is this so difficult for you?"

Her mouth got tight, which is never a good sign. "This is not so difficult for me," she snapped. "I'm just not sure what *you* would be happy with."

Oh, please. What would have made me happy, when Frank and I went to get the license was to have walked across the hallway and done the ceremony right there. But New York has a most inconvenient twenty-four-hour waiting period and it ended up being easier to go through with our original plans than to get all the way downtown again.

So, I admit that on the blushing-bride front I had not been cooperative. I gave myself a one-day limit to find the dress. I did. I agreed to use Rabbi Grauer, my parents' rabbi, but only because he is exceptionally cool. Frank and I met him for a drink near *The New York Times*, where we both work, and when he discovered that Frank didn't have a Hebrew name, gave him one right there in the bar. (Okay, so it's not partying with Mick Jagger, but for an Orthodox rabbi, it qualifies.)

Then we insisted that only immediate family and close friends (ours, not our parents') be invited. There went the neighborhood. "What will I tell them all?" my mother demanded. "They invited us to *their* daughter's wedding."

"Okay, Mom. Tell them I'm a horrible person who had the nerve to grow up and want something different than you."

This merited a tight mouth supreme. Her lips totally disappeared.

All of which explained this little costume parade on Wedding Day, her not-so-silent protest. She had *wanted* that bandleader to play "Hava Nagila," she had *wanted* the third cousins from Brooklyn to fight over who took the centerpiece home, she had *wanted* the little matchbooks that said FRANK AND ALEX so she could leave them lying around the house as a tangible reminder that finally (thank God!) I was actually someone's wife, part one of my manifest destiny completed. And I was depriving her.

Phoebe sorted through the pile of clothes; eventually we all agreed on a lavender cocktail dress that looked wonderful with pearls. Very mother-of-the-bride. And once that was accomplished, we all just sat. The apartment was in complete disarray (I was moving, after all), and, sitting in my slip, I went through checklists of details I had managed to write down on the backs of envelopes. This is not the way I thought it would be. For years, my half-baked fantasy of the day I got married was set at a place like Elizabeth Arden. The three of us, surrounded by white wicker furniture, would have our temples massaged and our toenails buffed as we sipped iced tea through straws, careful not to disrupt our lipstick.

Oh, well. I took two aspirin and lit a cigarette.

But I did get my wish in one way. I never wanted to walk down an aisle and I didn't. I walked through a freezer.

Before the ceremony, Phoebe and I were sequestered in the basement of the restaurant, in the owner's office—no windows, no air—while up above the noise of the arriving guests grew increasingly louder. I went to the bathroom for the hundredth time.

"Come with me, will you?" I asked Phoebe, and she did, straightening my dress, fussing with the veil, practically clucking. Even though she is my little sister, we both know how to take turns being Mommy when Mommy's not there. (Mommy made the wise choice of staying upstairs to greet the guests and belt a few vodkas.) But a fleet of Mommies couldn't help me now.

"I can't breathe," I said, panicked. I realized it must be the veil. I had it dyed the same shade as my dress and now it was poisoning me. My God! After all these years being convinced I would never fall in love, never get married, I finally do and I'm dying. My veil is murdering me and will be buried with me. (It should be buried with me, actually. The damn thing cost enough.)

"What time is it? What's taking so long?" I asked Phoebe. I didn't tell her I was dying. It might ruin the party. "What if we just left?"

"Everything is fine," she said. "It's almost six-fifteen, they're all sitting down, it's going to start any minute."

"No! It can't! I have to go to the bathroom!"

Finally, it was time. Phoebe took me by the hand, a strong, warm hand, and led me up the back stairs to the kitchen. I followed her feet, looking down, trying to concentrate on breathing. I began to notice it was cold. We had stopped in the freezer, waiting while the crowd up front was fine-tuning the *chuppa*. (That's the cloth attached to four poles that is held over the couple's heads to signify that they will always have shelter. With better insulation, I hope.)

I looked at Phoebe. Over her shoulder sat rows and rows of pale guinea hens with the same clammy goose bumps I had. "Oh, my God," I said.

She squeezed my hand. "Everything is fine," she told me soothingly. I didn't believe her. What if we got locked in here? It would be like that *Lucy* episode when she came out covered in icicles. I would die with icicles *and* pimples. Life is never fair.

"You look beautiful and you're in love," Phoebe said. "Come on." She led me past chefs in white jackets who all smiled, though they seemed terribly far away, and into the room where I saw my two incipient stepsons, Nat and Simon, who were then eleven and seven.

"Hi, you guys," I said, so calmly I almost looked behind me to see who it was.

Then it began. I still couldn't breathe. I sort of saw Mom on the outskirts of the *chuppa*, which was held by Dad and Greg (Emmett was taking finals at Stanford and couldn't come) and Frank's father and stepfather. I felt myself sway. But, lucky for me, I was not Rabbi Grauer's first swaying bride. He locked eyes with me, willing me to look only at him. And he knew! Without saying a word he lifted my veil, dispersing the poisonous gases and suddenly, it felt ten degrees cooler. Then I got to kiss my husband, and he stepped on the glass and I can honestly say I hardly remember anything else. Except relief. Exquisite relief. I could breathe!

More than a year passed. I was happy, but as I said, this marriage thing did get in the way of our Girls Only nights. The full family saw each other often, but it wasn't the same.

Then, one day, right before Christmas, I was talking to Mom on the phone about nothing in particular and she started to cry.

I was taken aback. She is not a crier.

"Mommy, what's wrong?" I asked, panicked.

"Oh, nothing," she said, trying to backtrack.

"Nothing? Are you kidding? Why are you crying?"

And she very reluctantly started to tell me about her stomach, which always gives her problems, precisely because she's not a crier and makes it a matter of pride to keep a stiff upper lip and persevere while others fall around her. But after some perseverance of my own, she finally relented and spilled the details.

This particular year, it seemed, money was tight, and she and my father hadn't taken a summer vacation, which is crucial for her. She works as a college professor and administrator, she's always been on a school schedule and summer is her favorite season. She loves the sun and the beach and she hadn't had it, so she was worn out. And to top it off, it was the Christmas season, which just stinks intrinsically, no matter how many halls you deck. Even with menorahs.

I tried regaling her with tales of holiday cheer.

"There's a Clinique bonus at Bloomingdale's!" I announced. Barely a murmur in response.

"*The Red Shoes* is on at midnight." A faint "Oh?"

"I saw that woman from temple on Madison Avenue and you'd never believe it, but she had her face lifted *again*." When all that got was a halfhearted "Really?" I knew the trouble was deep.

Here's where being the eldest separates the men from the boys, as it were. As we know, the oldest child is the most responsible child. We are the ones who are old enough to know better. We are the ones who show good judgment and keep our parents proud. We are the fix-it, cure-all, surrogate parent of our parents.

Oh, they deny it. They say that only they are the grown-ups, the responsible ones. But I've never met an eldest child who, sooner or later, didn't face a parent staring back at him or her in a frantic search for answers. Ever hear the saying that people in show business will listen to anybody? Same with parents. And when they're fed up with Aunt Minnie, Dr. Spock or the lady next door, the one they look to is you. *Now* what?

I tried to think, conjuring solutions. Of course, in my rush to mother my mother, I didn't stop to ask myself what I was doing. Or why. I was grown up now, married and a stepmother. I had a whole other family to take care of. Why was I still running to fix things for Mom? Because I always have? Yes. What power! When a parent, your ultimate authority figure, says, "Can you help me?" and you can, is there a bigger rush? Talk about being taken seriously. And so here I was, hearing that call the way a dog hears a whistle in the next county. After all, I told myself, it's only fair. Parents help their children all the time, which is okay because children are supposed to need help. Parents are supposed to magically know how to do everything, but, as I'm finding out myself, parents (and stepparents) are only children who got older. No one really has a clue.

When I was about four, I made up a list of my skills and went door-to-door in our neighborhood looking for buyers. I'm not sure what else I offered, but I do remember that "problem solving" cost two cents. No one took me up on it but Mom. And I've been doing it ever since, free of charge.

As she rallied now and made small talk, embarrassed by her outburst, I kept thinking: what would make her feel better? A vacation. Well, I didn't have that much time. How about a weekend? What would she like? A spa, probably, though who had the money? Florence? Paris? Sure, why not. She loves museums. Museums! Ah. The Stanhope appeared like a dream.

After years of our visiting the Metropolitan Museum of Art, I had come to consider the Stanhope Hotel, across the street on Fifth Avenue, an exhibit we would never get in to see. The volunteers at the museum's information desk always recommend tea at the Stanhope, but after numerous attempts through the years, showing up in the lobby with Mom to find the six—count 'em—six tables perennially filled, I gave up.

Or thought I did. But any time I was in the area, there it was, mocking me, the resourceful New Yorker who couldn't even master a tea reservation. I started asking friends if they had ever stayed at the

Stanhope. None had. Actually, the closest most had come was eating at its highly touted sidewalk café. They hadn't made it inside either.

But an editor at the *Times* had asked if I wanted to try reviewing a hotel—usually I write profiles for the Home and Living sections—and this would be the perfect time to do it. Weekends are tight since I became a stepmom; I'm with the kids. But in January, Frank was going to Washington on business for a week and I would be at liberty.

Well, Mom loved the idea. We could go to the Met and we would finally have our tea and drink it too. Of course we'd have to wait a few weeks until after the holidays, which was perfect incentive to live through New Year's Eve. Problem solved.

When Phoebe heard about our plan, she was livid. "What about me?" she demanded. "I want to go too."

"But I haven't had any time with Mommy since I got married," I protested.

"I haven't had time with you either," she countered.

I hadn't quite thought of that. Actually, I hadn't thought about Phoebe in a while. Being a decade younger had always meant that there would be long periods when we didn't see each other, and when we did, we were both focused on getting Mommy's approval. Or at least I was. As we got older, I realized that Phoebe was also focused on getting *my* approval. I guess it's logical. I mean, ten years doesn't sound like much now, but when I was a freshman in college, she was in third grade. Even then she would write to me asking my advice on her strategy for hooking a boyfriend. And I would give it to her, along with advice on everything else.

Now that we were older, thirty-four and twenty-four, respectively, and she was living around the corner from me, I began to see the possibility of our actually becoming friends, not just assuming she would be the Greek chorus for Mom and me. But I admit that in the midst of getting married and moving and still taking primary responsibility for the psychic care and feeding of Mommy, establishing this friendship did not feel like a pressing priority. It's like that with family. You just figure they'll be there when you finally get around to paying attention. I thought about all of this and decided, okay, she could join us for everything except the sleeping-over part. Still huffy, she accepted.

I booked the weekend package, which included a two-room suite facing Fifth Avenue and free passes to the Metropolitan Museum of Art and the Guggenheim. Perfect.

When I arrived late on a Friday afternoon, Mom was already waiting in the lobby. She sat very straight on her chair in the corner, ankles crossed. She's still such a good girl.

Our suite overlooked Fifth Avenue, with a spectacular view of the museum and Central Park South skyline. The living room was very beige except for a large breakfront filled with books. "You can even take them with you," the bellman said enthusiastically. "Just mail them back when you're finished." A closer look at the shelves revealed Dante's Purgatory section of *The Divine Comedy* and Archibald Alison's *History of Europe during the French Revolution*. Thanks a lot.

Mom had brought standard postholiday reading: *You Can Heal Your Life*, a self-help book by Louise L. Hay. I took a peek. "Some Points of My Philosophy" it said. Number one: "We are each 100 percent responsible for all of our experiences." Well, thank you, Louise. No news there. I also know I'm responsible for everyone else's experiences. At least Mom's. At least most of the time. Some of the time?

Forget Dante. This purgatory is mine.

We headed to Gerrard's for cocktails, an open room at the back of the Stanhope lobby with wood-paneled walls and forest-green sofas. I immediately felt at home here. In Mom's house there is also a green couch. Granted, it is olive green and corduroy, which sounds hideous, but really isn't. The green couch in our family is not only a destination, but a state of mind. While other people pine for Bermuda, Phoebe and I pine for the green couch, our emotional respite from the outside world. On the green couch, Mom will rub my feet, light my cigarette, listen to my stories as if Scheherazade were telling them. On the green couch we watch *I Love Lucy*, eat tuna-fish sandwiches, study the fire in the fireplace.

When all four children are at home there are some pretty ugly moments over who gets to sit on the green couch. Thankfully, the boys don't come home as much as Phoebe and I do, so we try to share. But what every kid *really* wants, especially one with siblings, is to have Mommy all to herself.

And here in Gerrard's I have triumphed. This weekend is a green couch for both of us, a release from routine, a coddle-fest. Mom looked great. Her blonde hair was swept back from her killer cheekbones and perfectly symmetrical jaw. People pay money for this kind of face. (My cheekbones are identical, actually—after a week on diuretics.) Her brown eyes are smart and big, her smile wide. There are the tiniest of lines around her upper lip—from smoking, she warns Phoebe and me. We nod, without listening. Tonight, the other guests smoked freely here, in that European way where no one makes exaggeratedly pained expressions at the first curl of smoke. Those are more appropriate for the bill.

We met Phoebe to see the movie *Enchanted April*, which she had seen already and loved. We did too. Inspired by its Italian setting, we went to Orso, a restaurant in the theater district, near the *Times*, where we picked up our three-way yakking rhythm without missing a beat and sat for hours, eating, drinking and smoking. The only things missing from our usual nights were the green couch and our nightgowns. When it was finally time to leave, Phoebe went reluctantly home alone, while we headed off to our Fifth Avenue suite. I felt guilty, for all of ten seconds. It was me and Mom now.

At the hotel, she liked having the two rooms to choose from so she didn't have to smoke in the bedroom. She's fastidious about that sort of thing, smoking (not to mention entertaining gentlemen callers) in public rooms only. So we flopped on the couches in the living room and talked about, oh, just stuff. I told her about a jerk in the office, and she hated him immediately. I told her that I successfully duplicated her meatloaf recipe and she glowed. Whatever little victory or hurt I have in the world, I can bring back to her lap and she will gladly celebrate or kiss it and make it better. She loves being Mommy.

As I love being a daughter, seeing myself in the Mommy Mirror, asking if I'm the fairest of them all and hearing the resounding "Yes!" As a child, the rules of the mirror are easy. "Mommy, look at the ashtray I made for you in arts and crafts." Good girl. "Mommy, I spilled Coke on the living-room couch." Bad girl. As an adult, the Mommy Mirror invariably develops some funhouse distortions:

"Mommy, I want to marry someone who's not Jewish."

"Mommy, I want to move to California."

"Mommy, I'm not sure I want to have kids."

And you hear that "Yes!" grow less and less resounding.

But no matter. Every adult I know still looks in that mirror, still contorts him- or herself to match that image, to be the fairest of them all. And if not, she takes what she can get. When Grandma died, Mom said forlornly, "Now I have no one to tell when I do something good." As if no one else could ever look at her and see the same thing her mother could. And no one else could. Losing her mother meant losing the mirror in which my mother could recognize herself.

That mirror is the first place you learn what you look like. And it's almost impossible to break. As I get older, I notice that most of my conversations with Mom are about me. What I think, how I feel, what I do. I guess they always have been, and as a child I expected them to be. But now there are times I would like a more equal dialogue. She is less comfortable, though, when the tables are turned, so by tacit agreement, we don't turn them too often. Being a mommy, after all, means total authority—mythically elevated biology. Being a woman with human shortcomings is not nearly as attractive an option. And having an adult daughter with her own (read different) set of criteria about life, who's not shy to share, doesn't seem the greatest incentive to her opening up. Sometimes, her reticence bothers me and I push. But she's a strong girl. She pushes back.

It is actually the superb quality of her listening, though, not the talking, that has been her greatest gift to me. No matter what, at the end of the day I would come home from school and tell her any little thing and she would be endlessly interested, not only in what I was saying but how I was saying it. I could make her laugh or I could make her angry, all by how I described what had happened to me.

It was getting late in our suite. We changed into our nightgowns. Mom looked at mine, sighing. "Didn't I just buy you three new ones?" she asked, exasperated. "Come here. Which is this?"

Actually, I hadn't meant to bring this one, which is about ten years old, with a faded blue-and-white print. The hem is frayed and the weave around the shoulders is close to threadbare. This is just one of those female areas I have never succeeded in. Like fingernails. I'd much rather peel them than grow them. Anyway, T-shirts do just fine for sleeping, don't they? The only sustained interest I have ever seen a man have in lovely lingerie is in removing it as quickly as possible.

Mom, who does not approve of this philosophy, was wearing her customary delightful confection with ribbons and lace around the collar.

She took a closer look at mine. "Honestly, Alex," she said, which translates into "If you were still living in my house this thing would be sprayed with Endust, wiping windowsills."

"Well, it's clean," I protested.

"That's something," she retorted.

In the interest of harmony I decided not to remind her that she once bought a housecoat at B. Altman that came with matching pot-holders. Potholders! Is that the ultimate *Glamour* Don't, or what?

I slid all the way under the covers, obscuring her view of the offending garment. But sleep at the Stanhope proved difficult because the heating system made loud crackling noises. And Mom insisted on keeping the bathroom light on. A year or two ago, she tripped in her flip-flops on the way to the bathroom and fractured a rib. Which neither of us wanted her to do again tonight.

Finally, it was morning. We considered it the height of luxury to skip our makeup and go straight to the dining room for breakfast, as if we lived there. Since breakfast was part of our package, there was no bill, which only heightened the fantasy. Being surrounded by the soothing blue-green murals and Baccarat chandeliers without even picking up a hairbrush was a better high in its own way than getting all dolled up for dinner. And why worry who saw us? Everyone was from someplace else.

We went to the Met first, without Phoebe, who decided she wanted to sleep late. Mom's spirits had been lifting since yesterday and by now she had recovered her schoolteacher exuberance. Field trips make her heart grow fonder. And as long as I could keep her out of the Egyptian exhibit all would be well. Everything the Egyptians ever did is anthropological genius in her book, the mummies, the beaten gold, the linen, the tools. ("No, Mom, I had no idea the Eighth Dynasty was so remarkable! I thought they only killed Jews!")

Today, I felt like taking a break from ingenuity, mine included. But she forged ahead. Ever notice how those backless marble benches become the most comfortable places in the world when confronted with ancient civilizations? I wanted to go to the Costume Institute. The current exhibit was of Norman Norell dresses donated by Lauren Bacall. If the Egyptians really knew anything, they would have left hieroglyphic instructions on how to break through the glass and get one out.

Phoebe joined us at the Guggenheim, where I got instant vertigo. The floors were connected by a descending spiral. If you started at the top, it was like going down a toilet in slow motion. Circling, circling, the white walls rising up around you. Art? Where?

Finally, it was 2:00 P.M., when the Stanhope began its tea service. We arrived at 2:15, genuinely excited. At last!

When I booked our weekend package I was told that reservations for tea were taken only for parties of six or more. So we came early, to avoid more disappointment. We entered the six-table salon and found no sign of tea, just two men smoking cigarettes and reading the paper. We seated ourselves at a table for four. A waiter appeared. "I'm sorry, madam, but this table is reserved."

"I thought you only take reservations for six or more," I said. Nodding, he transferred us to a couch.

Fifteen minutes passed and still no tea. The two men were eating cheeseburgers.

God, they looked good. But I've had a weakness for tea sandwiches since my very first lunch at the Bird Cage with Mom. That was the restaurant at Lord & Taylor, where no one knew about cholesterol and the best triangle on the plate was date-nut bread and cream cheese.

"Remember that, Mom?" I asked in reverie. "Those sandwiches they used to call society sandwiches, when we went shopping?"

"This does not bode well," she said, ignoring me to search for the waiter.

"Will the two of you just chill?" said Phoebe impatiently. "He'll get here." She was still put out that she didn't sleep over, even though she got to sleep late. She ran a hand around her long, dark hair, pushing it away from her face. She's a beautiful girl, always has been. Her cheekbones are like Mom's and her nose is absolutely perfect, tilting up a little in profile, as does her upper lip. If she hadn't been so much younger than me, her looks might have been a problem.

I examined her outfit. I liked the skirt she had on. I always like her skirts and her shoes and everything else she wears. She has that special quality no one else in my family has, "an eye," which she honed on the Sotheby's program in London and at the Pace Gallery, where she works as an archivist. This also means she can make drop-dead outfits from the most dejected sales racks and that her apartment looks as if it belongs in a magazine, even though all the stuff in it is secondhand. At that moment I was wearing an old sweater of my husband's over an old sweater of my mother's and an old skirt of my own. And that's just what it looked like.

Her skirt was wine-colored and fell in folds.

"Can I have it?" I asked, feeling the material.

"Please," she snorted.

Finally, menus appeared and we ordered. Another fifteen minutes passed and the waiter returned with a tray of sandwiches, sodden, ice cold, tasting of the refrigerator. The smoked salmon seemed actually spoiled, though the chicken breast was okay once it thawed. Tomato, watercress and egg tasted identical, which was to say like wet bread.

It took another thirty minutes to be served scones, which were good, though the accompanying Devonshire cream came in a cloudy glass dish. Mom looked distressed. She could probably tell you exactly when that dish was washed last and from the look on her face the news would not be good. We passed on the cream and also skipped the tartlets, which we had seen from a distance. They looked varnished in unnatural colors. And I was starting to get a too-natural headache.

The long-awaited tea was a complete bust. The linchpin in my brilliant plan for Mom's emotional redemption. Now what?

"We should have had the cheeseburgers," Phoebe said.

"I know," I answered. "Maybe we should just go upstairs and rent a video." I was suddenly exhausted.

"Oh, the two of you," Mom said impatiently. Feeling a tantrum on the horizon (next we'd be fighting over which tape to rent), she steered us down Fifth Avenue into the Central Park Zoo. Not that either of us particularly loves zoos, but Mom does. Always has. I get the same feeling looking at a monkey sitting all alone, blinking, as I do watching the old men in black coats sitting all alone in the deli on Sunday night eating corned-beef sandwiches with their hats still on. It's not religion. They just forgot to take them off, and there's no one around to remind them.

But even at our ages, being supervised in a child's activity by Mom is deeply comforting. To all of us. Phoebe and I don't have to think. And Mom is once again in charge, her nominally adult daughters redeemed by her indisputably adult surefooted sense of New York and the human spirit. She grew up here. She drives here. She even used to wrap a kitchen knife in a yellow paper napkin and tuck it in her evening bag when we went to the theater at night. Don't mess with Mom.

So we were all happy now. My weekend started out to save my mother, and then, to preserve the natural order of things, my mother got to save the weekend. And once the weekend ceased being perfect, Phoebe got her revenge for not sleeping over.

We wandered. The polar bears swam laps. The monkeys all had company. The penguins dove and splashed. Our mood lifted.

The zoo was also the ideal break from all our luxury. The catch to vacationing in your own city is that it's disorienting. Even though you know exactly where you are, your home base is different and so is your focus, so you end up feeling the same uncertainty you do someplace foreign. It makes you tired.

We retreated to our room. Mom and Phoebe lay down on the bed.

"Ha-ha, I'm sleeping here anyway," Phoebe said, snuggling up to Mom's shoulder; who smiled and shook her head. I started to eat the Godiva mint chocolate left on the pillow the night before, and after Mom had closed her eyes, stuck my chocolate-covered tongue out at Phoebe.

"You are gross," she said.

"Stop it, Alex," Mom said, without opening her eyes.

While they slept, I sat near the window, looking out. It was late afternoon, and a winter twilight streaked the sky pink. The sound of the fountains in front of the museum was faint, but calming. A crowd milled under the big banners and two girls broke away, leaping down the stairs, their coats flying open, laughing. That forgotten teenage elation when it's almost Saturday night.

As it suddenly was. Phoebe left to go to a party, all scores settled. Mom and I had invited my friend Philip to join us for a room-service dinner. I wanted him to bring his German shepherd, Barney, but he didn't think the Baccarat crystal in the lobby would survive it. He brought some vodka instead and we ate in the sitting room and watched *Saturday Night Live* and talked and smoked and had a ball. Mom's life seemed healed without Louise Hay. At least for now.

After Philip left, Mom went to sleep. "Thank you, sweetheart," she whispered, before turning out the light. "I've had a marvelous time." And she hugged me, surrounding me with her great Mommy smell, the smell I remember as a child, of Joy perfume and soap and cigarettes and just a touch of Adorn hair spray. There's nothing better in the world.

I sat in the darkened living room, savoring the silence. It was almost 2:00 A.M. Mission accomplished, problem solved. Even Mom's stomach had remained dormant for the entire weekend. The ultimate achievement.

But sitting there then, I asked myself how the weekend was for me. Pretty good, actually. Then why did I feel so unsettled? Because I kept wondering what being a grown-up *means*. Was I one? I didn't feel like it. As long as my parents are alive, I guess I'll always be a child. Their child. An adult child—the oxymoron of the century. Aging child is more like it. With the luxury of aging parents, who still eat dinner at six every night, still watch the evening news, still drink their tea after that. I know just where they are at every minute of the day and when I call them I know they will answer.

I had been married for more than a year. Why didn't I feel different? Mom always called me the original Peter Pan and it's almost true. I never wanted to grow up, yet I couldn't wait to grow up. I never wanted to leave my family and I always wanted to leave my family. I wanted to fly away on astonishing journeys and wake up safe in my very own bed.

And it would seem I got my wish, because there I was, married— big life change—and nothing had changed. Mom and I were still here in our nightgowns escaping the boys in our life, and the boy parts of life, the ugly, grown-up, outside world rules and duties.

It flashed, then, the reason why I felt so stalled. I kept waiting to grow up, but at the same time I kept waiting to be a child. Not the oldest, the one who reads a library book a day, wins every spelling bee, shakes hands with adults and curtsies on cue. But another kind of child, one who drips her Popsicle on a clean white shirt, tears her new pants climbing a tree, calls out of turn in class and doesn't even know the answer. And not only lives to tell the tale but tells it while being unconditionally adored.

I had to laugh. If that was what I was waiting for, I would wait a long time. Like for my next life, maybe. Or the one after that.

Out the window, the museum was glorious in the night. The fountains were off, the pools of water shone. Utter tranquility. The stairs were perfectly stacked cubes of white. Cleaned of crowds, it was like a movie set, a majestic building I suddenly wasn't sure I had ever really seen before.

I noticed a light then, off to the left of the main entrance. I retraced our path from earlier that morning, trying to visualize where it was coming from.

Of course. Those damned Egyptians. Don't they ever sleep?

chapter two

Knowing Creamware

Once I got home I did a nightgown inventory, and except for three new additions from Mom, found that all the others were indeed ripped. Why should I be surprised? I had never bought nightgowns for myself because Mom bought them for me—probably because they were the only things I allowed her to buy. They were never an intrusion of taste the way a sweater or a blouse could be. (You expect me to wear *that*?) So, as the woman perennially in charge of my bedtime, I let her buy them all, including the ones identical to hers. And to Phoebe's. The Three Musketeers of the night. What did it matter? No one ever saw them but us.

Also, quite frankly, I was too cheap to spend money on clothes that no one would see. Which is how I'm not like Phoebe. Actually, it's one of 9,356 ways I'm not like Phoebe, who'll spend $90 on a black velour bathrobe just to wear while she's putting on her makeup. All I tend to wear are flannel Lanz nightgowns, which I fixated on as a student at Wheaton College, in Norton, Massachusetts. Everyone there wore them, turned backward with the buttons in the front. Very preppie. Especially with a turtleneck underneath for cold nights. As nightgowns go, they truly are the epitome of asexuality. Sort of like the lining of a sleeping bag.

But they still remain my nightgowns of choice. I can answer the door in one and tip the delivery guy from the butcher without being embarrassed. I can also wear one to cook the kids' breakfast on the weekend without setting off any prepubescent step-oepedipal firecrackers. But, after fifteen years of continual service, perhaps it was time for a new one (okay, maybe a few new ones). Perhaps (horrors!) it was even time for me to buy them for myself.

I extended my inventory to sweaters, putting them all out on the bed and counting. Almost half were still from college. And almost half of those were Fair Isle—you know, with that pattern around the neck. Well, I had certainly been economical. As Mom always advocated, I had treated my clothes properly and they had lasted. But maybe this was a little crazy. Should I really be pushing middle age and wearing the same clothes I took my SATs in?

So when the *Times* offered another assignment away from my beat—shopping at Bergdorf Goodman—I said yes, and immediately recruited Phoebe for the job. My plan was not to buy there, but like all the brides I knew, see what they had and then go to Kleinfeld's in Brooklyn for the knockoff. My version of the knockoffs would come from catalogue shopping, an obsession I picked up from Mom, since it had the added benefit of being a green-couch activity. Bergdorf would show me styles of today, New York circa 1993, instead of Norton, Mass., circa 1975.

Now, I can't say exactly when it was that Phoebe started knowing better than me about clothes, but it came as something of a shock that she did. I remember, at the tender age of five, accompanying my father's mother, whom we called Nana, on a shopping expedition, where I picked out a long black coat for her with shiny black buttons. Well, from her ecstatic reaction to my excellent taste, you would have thought I was the Coco Chanel of the kindergarten. I certainly did. The same thing happened with Mom. Not that I picked out her clothes, but she always let me pick out my own. I learned decision making in department stores. When I was growing up, we would shop at Alexander's and because we couldn't afford two dresses I would have to pick one. And Mom would crow over my brilliant taste. The choice was always right and I would leave feeling that I had purchased the single most important outfit in the entire store. Each one was so important, in fact, that we would name them. My favorite was the British Tea Dress. It had a checked pattern in olive and cream, a full skirt and a bodice with lace at the throat and on the sleeves, along with black velvet trim. No one I knew had a dress as lovely, and I figured that, with my eye, I would grow up to become a world-famous dress designer. Alexandra. Of Alexander's.

I was in college when I realized that Phoebe not only knew how to dress (at the age of eight), but she also knew, remarkably, how to put on makeup and, even more remarkably, how to get away with murder with my father, being sweet and feminine and drooling "Daddy" at him. Scarlett O'Harawitz.

Phoebe could also accessorize my mother's outfits better than my mother could. And she could go to her closet and find two things that looked crazy together until Mom put them on, and then suddenly she would have a brand-new outfit that would never have occurred to her. When she was in the ninth grade, Phoebe bought a pair of red flats with gold trim. Mom was furious because they cost a lot and they wouldn't go with anything. Well, sonofabitch, they went with everything. I don't know how—on me they never would have—but on her they did.

It was a few years later that Phoebe mastered the "It's too late now" strategy, of which she remains the reigning champion. On a family vacation to Jamaica, when she was fourteen, Phoebe disappeared for hours and returned with a head full of beaded cornrows. She had found some woman on the beach to do it for her, and I think my parents were so relieved she hadn't come back with a head full of ganja that they just let it go. Phoebe didn't wash her hair for two weeks so she didn't mess it up, dipping Q-tips in alcohol and running them along her scalp instead.

To let this happen was a supreme sacrifice for Mom in the motherly love department, since in her book cleanliness surpasses godliness every time. As we were growing up she told us that if we did not wash our hair regularly, it would get up and walk off our heads. I don't have to tell you how fervently I believed her. A boy I knew in high school once said that the first thing he thought of when he thought about me was how clean my hair was.

"Can you believe that?" I asked Mom. "Out of everything to remember about someone, that was all he could think of."

She was unmoved. "So? Would you rather he remember it was dirty?" she asked.

When Phoebe was bat mitzvahed she received about twenty gold-chain necklaces, the "in" gift from girls of her grade, and she put on all twenty at once, hopelessly tangling them. Mom went through the roof on that one. She threatened that she would take her to the jeweler and have them all cut off and Phoebe yelled and screamed, clearly terrified that Mom was mad enough to have the jeweler cut her head off too. But Mom calmed down and made Phoebe sit still for hours while she picked out every knot in those chains with a needle. Next to the time Gregory choked on a fishbone when he was three and Mom frantically stuffed him with bread to get it to go down, this particular activity was the best argument I could think of for not having children.

Then one afternoon when no one was home, Phoebe appealed to a neighbor's mother who was handy with a paintbrush to come over and paint a huge bright purple zigzag on three of her light-blue bedroom walls, one of which proclaimed PHOEBE. Mom went speechless on that. My father, who had paid virtually no attention to the hair revolution or the necklace binge, stood at Phoebe's bedroom door growing apoplectic as the realization dawned that to change it now, he'd have to pay for it. It stayed. But she had to coo an awful lot of "Daddy"s over that one.

Whenever Phoebe did one of these things, I would overhear my parents' clandestine comments about her that ranged from "artistic" to "excessive" to "crazy" in tones that ranged from dismissive to analytic to contemptuous. I wanted no part of that. Phoebe might be a genuine risktaker, but I stuck with "smart," "reliable" and "responsible," all virtues strongly endorsed by Mom. I liked being safe. Good. A good girl.

And like Mom, I was never rash, tending instead to deliberate every decision to death. When I was twelve I took the giant leap and cut my hair from waist-length to a pixie and was traumatized every minute of the three years it took to grow back. For my bat mitzvah I was also given jewelry, but there is some of it I still haven't worn. Two enamel butterfly pins to be exact, which are meant to go on an overcoat (what if it rains?) and so, have stayed protected in their box. As for decorating my bedroom, the most daring attempt I ever made was a big sign on the door that said KEEP OUT.

Anyway, Phoebe, with her utter disregard for rules combined with her great eye, is an ideal shopping partner. She also has stamina and patience once she enters a store that are in inverse proportion to mine.

I don't know when shopping changed for me. When I was a kid, department stores were among my favorite places. They seemed the ultimate in sophistication, with endless varieties of lipsticks and hats on the ground floors, where it always smelled as if a movie star had just walked by. Then, up the escalator, would be glittering evening gowns and velvet evening coats and peau de soie pumps that felt like ribbons.

And lunch, in either the Bird Cage at Lord & Taylor or Charleston Gardens at B. Altman. For a while, Bloomingdale's had some Swedish conceit of open-faced sandwiches, but that didn't really work because by the time you were back among the Baccarat, you were starving again.

In the last few years the department stores have begun to disappear. I think I miss the violets on the Bonwit Teller bag most. They meant luxury and luck, since I could almost always find what I wanted there.

I also miss a certain type of merchandise, things like the three-tiered Lenox candy dishes B. Altman used to sell. What an idea. No one even eats candy anymore. At least not in public. Mom mourns B. Altman regularly. "I miss that store," she'll say sternly, as if waiting for someone to present a case for closing it. When silence ensues, she'll sigh. And say it was the kind of place where you could buy silver polish and Princess Borghese makeup, sensible shoes and chiffon, all at once. (Not to mention a housecoat with potholders. Where else could you find that? Kmart?)

I must admit I felt partially responsible for the department stores' demise, having turned catalogue junkie. And I mean catalogues for everything, dishes, shoes, even toothpaste. The freedom of fantasy you get with a catalogue can be heady. Just turn down the corner of every page where you sort of like something, and you can pretend you've bought it. When I am actually free to go shopping, say on a Saturday afternoon, I'm expert at finding excuses not to. Once you learn to shop lying down, it's too hard to get up again.

But I planned on triumphing at Bergdorf's, waking up to a whole wide world of grown-up fashion without once thinking of hemming something for "room to grow." And the benefit of Bergdorf's is that it's guaranteed to be less frenetic than Bloomingdale's, since its ultra-exclusive attitude terrifies more people than it tantalizes. Or maybe it just terrifies me. My relationship with Bergdorf's has always been erratic. It was probably my first trip there, at twelve, when Mom and I were looking for my bat mitzvah dress that set the standard. Trying to impress upon me the vast difference between this store and Alexander's, she proclaimed that Bergdorf's was so expensive I would probably only shop there again when I got married. That sounded serious. A little too serious, actually. We bought the dress at Bonwit Teller.

Not that I would have minded buying it at Alexander's. We used to go to the one in Paramus, New Jersey, with the huge mural on the outside, and I loved it. It had a superior tuna-fish sandwich and a Coke with not too much ice, and the grown-up dresses there were the greatest. My favorite was covered with bright emerald green spangles the size of quarters, almost flapper style. I thought Mom was making the mistake of a lifetime when she refused to buy it. It looked like the kind of jazzy dress a nightclub singer would wear, like Petula Clark singing "Downtown." Mom didn't seem to consider that a plus.

By the time I hit the seventh grade and left New Jersey for Scarsdale, I'm sorry to say that the Alexander's in nearby White Plains became a destination for my friends and me to shoplift bikini panties. They were ninety-nine cents each and it was all the rage on a Saturday afternoon to slip a pair into your purse. I was too chicken to take more than a few, especially after one of my best friends got so inspired she included a tennis racket in her haul and the store detectives landed on her as she tried to make an exit. Not only did she get in trouble, but her parents made her see a shrink. Which in retrospect maybe wasn't so terrible, because she liked it so much she became one herself.

Many, many years after seventh grade I even dated one of the numerous offspring of the family that owned Alexander's. He was an owlish fellow whom I rather liked at the beginning. After we met he sent an enormous bouquet of balloons to my office, which was quite sweet, though you can imagine my bewilderment when he forgot our next date. When he remembered, we ended up at a restaurant called Memphis, a terribly "in" place in 1980s New York with an unmarked entrance, Cajun food, a desperate bar scene and awful noise. Everything you could want in a romantic evening and more—blackened redfish on your breath and no clue what your date is saying.

During dinner, the retailing heir left the table for quite some time and returned with a bottle of Afrin and an elaborate story about allergies. Then he informed me solemnly that since highly desirable single women like me did not have a long shelf life in the current market, he thought it best that I enter into a relationship with him immediately. Which, he added, would not preclude his continuing the one he was already in. I pondered my shelf life and decided I must already be on sale to get an offer like this.

To his surprise, I turned him down and didn't hear from him again for months. Then an invitation arrived to his annual Christmas party, which was a zoo of people crammed into his Greenwich Village loft. And I thought, good, maybe I can go and find someone else who won't notice my expiration date, since I was still (shamefully) unattached. I showed up with a friend, much to the heir's horror, and I could see instantly that he had simply forgotten to delete my name from his computerized Rolodex. So I smiled a lot, had a few drinks and left just as the coat racks collapsed, sending all the fun fur onto the dusty concrete floor. On the way home my thoughts turned to tennis rackets. I should have taken them all while I still had the chance.

Back to Bergdorf's. It's not that I've purposely avoided shopping there. It's just that the key to hiding the fact that you have no money for clothes is either to have impeccable taste, or, failing that, to wear lots of black. I would go for the sales, where I had two great victories:

a black evening blouse for $25 that still looks terrific nine years later, and a pair of Charles Jourdan pumps for my wedding. (See, Mom, you were right! Even though I got the dress in SoHo and deprived you of the Kleinfeld's experience, I ended up at Bergdorf's anyway. Two days before the wedding, actually. My checklists somehow never encompassed shoes.)

In recent years I've made a truly crucial discovery that also keeps me connected to Bergdorf's: there is never a line at its Clinique counter. Other women I know go to the Frédéric Fekkai Beauty Center, also at Bergdorf Goodman, a place so rarefied I had only read about it, and which achieved world-class status when its owner sheared Hillary Rodham Clinton. Mere mortals wait at least three months for an appointment with Mr. Fekkai for a haircut that costs close to $300, if you please. But a friend who has her nails done there says the salon always gives her a lift.

Well, I'd never had a manicure. And Phoebe had never had a pedicure. So that would be her prize for shepherding me through the racks. Not that she needed the incentive.

"Hi, Phoebe? Could you possibly come shopping with me? I have to go to Bergdorf's to do a story and—"

"Cool," she said. "Will they pay for what we buy?"

"Are you kidding?"

Silence. She's never been one for rhetorical questions. She was waiting for me to say yes.

"No, Phoebe, they will not pay. If we buy, we pay ourselves."

"Bummer."

"Will you come anyway?"

"Sure. No big deal."

Only for me. I felt I was going camping in Africa. But Phoebe had inherited the dominant shopping gene from Grandma, my mother's mother. Grandma was incredibly beautiful, with jet black hair, ivory skin and the kind of shocking green eyes men write about. She also

happened to be 5'2", 180 pounds. But those were the days when everyone was fat and neither she nor anyone else seemed to mind. Before she
got married she worked as a milliner (she had the eye before Phoebe
did) and everything she owned was pretty, from her teacups to her lin-
ens. She used to show me shapes and characters in the pattern of our
bathroom wallpaper that I could never find myself. Ever since she died
in 1982, Mom has kept her dress-up blouse, a dramatic print with gold
threads through it, hanging in her own closet.

Grandma shopped like breathing. Even in the months before she
died, I remember her on the phone to Macy's, haranguing someone
over a late delivery. As her spiritual retailing heir, Phoebe also shops
nonstop. Depending on her mood, she'll even buy things she can't remotely afford. Lizard cowboy boots for $600? Sold.

I shop like Mom. Every purchase has a reason, every separate has
a mate, every shoe an identically colored bag. I also tend to buy in
bulk—just in case. Shoes that fit well? I get the same style in every
color (a Mom trick). I'll also buy things like toilet paper, Scott towels,
aluminum foil in huge quantities. Just in case. Just in case what? The
urge to broil strikes at midnight? Mom's house, same story. She has a
full freezer in the garage to hold all her culinary just-in-cases. And the
basement? Don't ask.

But my credit card bills, like Mom's, are always paid in full. Phoebe's carry. I almost never see anything I like. Phoebe likes everything
she sees. I buy black, she buys what she wants and if she doesn't know
what goes with it, she doesn't care, she'll figure it out later. When
Frank once told me to stop obsessing and just buy some new clothes
already, Phoebe turned to him, shimmering with emotion. "I hope I
marry a man just like you," she said.

Of course, I would never let my husband pay for my clothes. Mom
never did either. I am an adult, I can dress myself (except for Mommy
still buying my nightgowns). Phoebe has no use for this mutually ex-

clusive philosophy of men and financial independence. Neither did Grandma, who spent her husband's money happily—he was one of the first to sell nylon stockings in the Bronx, so she had some to spend. Phoebe alighted upon her rich-husband philosophy at a very young age. It didn't matter that Mom was career a-go-go. It didn't matter that I was too. She just wasn't and didn't want to be. From the beginning, she loved the idea of babies, lunch at the club and new clothes in the closet. And Mom and I couldn't help but reinforce her housewifely scheme once we saw her work Daddy, because it was such an impressive show. For instance: When I was in seventh grade, I would get into bloody battles with him about wearing a hat. He was very big on us wearing hats in cold weather, since so much of your body heat escapes through your head and he didn't want us to get sick. So, on a frigid day, he would insist I ruin my hair by putting on a hat while I waited at the bus stop. The nerve!

Phoebe was not exempt from the hat rule, but Phoebe never wore a hat. She didn't refuse. She didn't argue. What an incredible waste of time and energy! Phoebe smiled. Phoebe simpered. Phoebe agreed. Yes, she had her hat. Yes, she was putting it on. Yes, she knew it would keep her warm. And when my father drove his car out of the driveway, he would look out the window to see Phoebe at the front door wearing her hat. Satisfied, off he would go. And as soon as the car disappeared, she would double back into the front hallway, take off the hat, redo her hair and go merrily on her way. No tears. No battles of will. And, looking fabulous, she would sweep into homeroom and start the day right.

Daddy aside, Phoebe did okay with guys, though she got off to a slow start. First of all, she was always tall, a real killer, especially in junior high when all the boys are peanuts. Also, she was not only pretty, she always looked older than she was. I remember when Neiman Marcus opened in White Plains (replacing the only other Bergdorf Goodman, actually) and Mom and I heard that the restaurant there was so

fancy-shmancy that the women of Westchester were making reservations for lunch. This struck us both as hysterically funny and we immediately did the same for the three of us. Phoebe was twelve or thirteen
at the time.

We decided that we would all wear hats for the big lunch. Mom
had her mother's milliner gene and the top shelf of her closet was filled
with hatboxes. She rationalized it (as of course she would have to) as
being a necessity for her annual guest appearances in temple on the
High Holidays.

That day, she wore one that made me crazy, white with a huge
white feather, à la Robin Hood. I took one that was fedora-style with a
band of multicolored feathers and Phoebe had a plain, wide-brimmed
navy number, some sort of suede, I think. We all wore identical
button-down blouses and A-line skirts with boots, very seventies. I'm
sure we thought we looked like Charlie's Angels.

But when we arrived at the restaurant and announced our reservation, we were the only ones laughing. The women who were hatless
looked stricken by their own careless omission. The women behind us,
who hadn't reserved and had to wait behind a velvet rope, wrung their
hands and shook their heads with self-loathing. As if the chance to eat
this chicken salad was akin to gaining admission to Studio 54.

When we were immediately seated and the incredibly preten-
tious waiter approached asking if we wanted white wine, he automatically included Phoebe. She hadn't graduated from eighth grade,
but even then she was taller than I was and in that hat, with her
cheekbones, looked sort of like Charlotte Rampling. Poor thing.
Not poor thing that she looked good, but that everyone, Mom and
I included, would forget that she was just a little kid. And when
Mom would say something Phoebe didn't understand and Phoebe
would look blank or say "What?" Mom would turn very impatient
and snap her fingers and say, "Quick on the uptake," like she would

say to me, because she wanted her children alert and brilliant and extraordinary. Right now.

The fact that Phoebe was not as intellectually predatory as Mom— or me—didn't matter seriously because she was always smart. It's just that her focus was different. She didn't give a shit if she didn't know the answer *first*. She knew what she wanted to know. Period. Like, when it came to reading, a family mandate, Phoebe didn't. Wouldn't. Refused. I bought her *A Tree Grows in Brooklyn*, the ultimate girl-growing-up book, and to this day she hasn't opened it.

For a while she painted. She brought home a painting of the ocean done all in pinks and purples that was the most exquisite thing you had ever seen a sixth grader do in your life. So exquisite in fact that Mom had it framed. Dad raved, we all ogled it. Phoebe never painted again. I don't know why. She doesn't know why. Or says she doesn't. I think she was refusing to play the achievement game, which was our family's daily sweepstakes. While I slaved for A's, Phoebe said, in essence, Fuck you. I'm your child, I'm your sister and you can love me for just doing nothing or not at all. Pretty brave, in fact. I couldn't do it. I still can't.

Why are we so different? Only the DNA knows for sure. Or maybe, underneath it all, we're really alike only I'm repressed and she's not.

Phoebe always demanded that we hug her and kiss her (we didn't do much of that when I was growing up, since I think in the fifties experts advised against it). While everyone else in our family woke up in a bad mood, she awoke sunny and refreshed. Then, of course, she would go to school and stand on the desks and shout, disrupting the entire class, until they called Mom. And then she would stop. Phoebe's position has always been "Take me or leave me," knowing someplace deep where it matters that we'll take her every time. Or most of the time.

When I started to know Phoebe as an adult, I was struck by this basic difference between us, and though I admired it, never aspired to imitate her. Still, I was drawn to her blatant emotionalism, her great loyalty and yes, her unyielding obsession to get my approval along with Mom's. It's flattering to have a little semi-you hanging on your every word. Our dynamic was a combination of personality differences and the shared experience of family life. Our references were the same. Our approaches differed. But we always liked each other.

For a few years in college, Phoebe had a serious boyfriend, but not since. She goes out a lot ("Practice your dating skills!" Mom cries) but an Onassis has yet to appear. When he does, I hope he has a good lawyer.

Finally, our shopping day arrived. Bergdorf's sits across the street from the Plaza Hotel, and next to the Paris movie theater, which is always showing something arty and chic. These three places share a small corner of New York that never disappoints in its sheer glamour quotient. Inside Bergdorf's the motif is one of quiet opulence—until you see the price tags, which is when the screaming starts.

On the ground floor I was reassured to see the standard lone woman buying Clinique. A peek inside the Judith Leiber boutique revealed a variety of eccentrically designed handbags, including a jeweled pig's head. A noisy return was in progress, leaving the distinct impression that the customer bought a bag expressly for last night, and now, in the cruel light of morning, doesn't want to pay for it. Phoebe smiled. Done that, been there.

We wandered. Exceptionally tall models struck poses in their outfits, holding the designer's name on cards. None of them made eye contact. They hovered nearby with odd, predatory looks. Maybe they were just hungry.

I could use a new shoulder bag, actually. The one I liked was by Isaac Mizrahi and cost $590. Or I could buy a new shoulder.

On the second floor I was quickly hypnotized by a pair of Manolo Blahnik navy loafers for $395. A woman tried on a pair, her schnauzer tucked under her arm. She bought them. I hated her. Phoebe shrugged.

Up another flight we found a honeycomb of designer alcoves off the main hall. But I was afraid to walk inside any of them. I found myself expecting a museum-type alarm to go off if I got too close to the clothes. The sale racks were easier to approach, orphaned in the hallways between the alcoves. I dove through one and saw a Jean Muir navy silk sweater marked down from $865 to $259. For Ivana Trump, this was probably some deal.

The store was filling up now, and the predominant customers seemed to be impeccably preserved middle-aged women with no discernible jobs or appointments, judging from their gait and rhythm. But each one was dressed to take over a major corporation at a moment's notice.

I considered this strange. Phoebe did not. "This is their business," she explained. "To shop. And when they get here they are greeted by someone behind a desk. These women are going to work."

Really? How come my guidance counselor never presented this as an option?

We skipped to the fifth floor for coffee, where there was also an affordable shoe department. Actually, the whole floor was more affordable than the others. And then I saw it. A pure white Calvin Klein cotton sweater. Poetry. It conjured long weekends amid dunes and sea spray, wispy clouds floating above. The price? $34. My heart pounded. I picked it up to try on and saw the price was really $150. The T-shirt lying on the table next to it was $34. Okay, so what? I held it in front of me. It looked a little big. Phoebe was off at another rack. Fine, I could do this alone. The sea spray beckoned and I savored it there at the mirror.

Aren't I worth it?

Of course.

What if it's too big?

That's the look.

It's white, it goes with everything.

It's cotton, I can't wear it past September.

Maybe it's not a good investment.

Maybe it doesn't have to be an investment.

It would look great with leggings at a cocktail party in the Hamptons.

I hate the Hamptons.

Right. Which means I'll be staying in the city, where I always spend my weekends, with the kids, ketchup and cookie-dough ice cream. I put it back. Phoebe was disgusted.

Thankfully, it was time for my maiden manicure, the affordable pampering of the day. The Frédéric Fekkai salon was on the seventh, and top, floor, past the housewares and gifts. On the way I fell deeply, passionately in love with a bone-colored tea set, which Phoebe identified as Creamware, made in Leeds.

"How can you possibly know that?" I demanded.

"Because I spent a year in London on that Sotheby's course. I had to learn about ceramics."

You know, the thing about being an older sister, especially a ten-years-older sister, is that you tend to never believe anything a younger sister says. She couldn't possibly know better than you about anything. You knew everything first. And because of that she always looks up to you, and as a really big favor you deign to share whatever little nuggets of wisdom you've picked up along the way—she's such an innocent—and that's that.

I turned over a teacup. LEEDS, it read. Amazing.

"Is it expensive?" I asked. "How come there's not a price on it?"

"If there's not a price, it's expensive. Come on, we'll be late."

I saw a saleslady.

"Excuse me!" I blasted.

She came over. "Yes?"

"Do you know how much this is?"

She peered at the set. "Well, I think the creamer is $145, but I can check on the whole thing." There must have been thirty pieces.

"Oh, thank you so much, that's okay." I started to burble. "It's a gift, and I think I already know what I'm going to buy instead."

She walked away.

"Told you," Phoebe said.

"Shut up," I replied, pulling open the double glass doors to Frédéric Fekkai.

At the front desk were two bored blondes dressed in black. "Can I help you?" asked one, barely looking up.

"Yes," I answered.

She looked up all the way and smiled beatifically, suddenly welcoming. I smiled back. Maybe she was nearsighted and I misunderstood her initial ennui. "Hello," she purred, going right past me, practically into Nancy Reagan's arms. Mrs. Reagan was accompanied by two Secret Service agents who were having a hard time trying to look menacing while being surrounded by blondes bearing iced tea.

"I'm so sorry I'm late," she said graciously before being whisked to the dressing room to put on a robe for her appointment with Mr. Fekkai. The blonde, bored again, trudged through the salon and pointed at a vacant spot where we were to sit and wait for Jeanette, the manicurist.

"How cordial," I said to Phoebe.

"Lovely," she responded.

The blonde trudged off.

And then we sat. While I glared at a woman wearing thick ribbed cashmere socks and glove-leather loafers, for no other reason except that I could afford neither, Phoebe started a conversation with an older-looking Leslie Caron type who said she just left a $500 lace top in a cab and hoped it would turn up soon. She seemed remarkably calm, leafing through *Cos-*

mopolitan and ordering an avocado salad, which was soon delivered on a tray. Then she made a phone call. I saw Phoebe mulling the notion of a $500 lace top and tried to ignore her, because with the slightest encouragement she might have to see what it felt like to buy one herself.

I looked around. My friend had promised that even if we didn't want lunch, someone would offer us coffee, or the use of the phone. Someone did not.

Finally, Jeanette fetched me. She was older, warm and reassuring. She sat near Mr. Fekkai's chair and the procession of customers walking by to check out Mrs. Reagan, while pretending not to, had begun. Actually, here, Mrs. Reagan did not look stick-thin. She looked like everyone else. And while the customers were obsessed with getting a good look at her, the employees were decidedly blasé. It was their policy never to pass a mirror without looking at themselves, a duty they performed lovingly.

Jeanette said I had good cuticles and thin nails. Twenty minutes later they gleamed. Yes, they looked pretty, but $26 plus tip? I had seen the future, and it did not include Jeanette.

While Phoebe had a pedicure, cotton woven through her toes à la Rita Hayworth, I took the Nancy Reagan tour. With the aid of a hand mirror, she was admiring some very lovely blonde highlights. Phoebe meanwhile had to keep sitting still, waiting for the whole production to set or dry or whatever it does. We were both starting to starve.

But, gallantly, we put shopping before food, the ultimate sacrifice, and because we had skipped the fourth floor, back we went, en route to lunch at the men's store, where I was told by a friend that the chicken potpie was sublime. On the fourth floor, where designer evening wear was sold, some of it behind glass, two clerks fought about a sale that got away.

"But then her husband said it was too dark," one said plaintively, holding the accused, a plum-colored satin gown. "Well, what did you say?" snapped the other. "I gave up," the first admitted, gloomily. Phoebe shook her head. Amateurs. This is a girl who has called stores across the country to track down a pair of shoes she absolutely had to have, and once she got them, wore them at least twice before they completely bored her and she wanted something else.

We arrived at the men's store at 2:30, after the lunch crowd. The menu here included corned beef on rye and meatloaf, neither of which was available at the women's store. Unfortunately, the room smelled like a cafeteria. And the word *sublime* did not belong in the same sentence, not even the same paragraph, with this chicken pie.

"I don't want to go back to work," I whined. "Do you?"

"I don't have to," Phoebe said. "I called in sick."

"You did? Don't you feel guilty?"

"No. Why should I?"

She was right, of course. It was all Mom's fault that I'm so honorable about every little thing. One day when I was seven Mom had picked up some dry cleaning, and was given a ten-dollar bill as change instead of a single.

"Wow, you made nine dollars," I crowed.

"No, I did not," she glared. "I am going right back in there to return this money. What will that man do at the end of the day when he realizes that he's lost nine dollars? He has a family to support. And what if this wasn't the only mistake he made?"

Well, she was right. But still. There are times when it seems that I spent my entire childhood as a Xerox machine stuck in overdrive. I did every exact thing right, as Mom instructed, so that it looked just like her. But even though my first-grade teacher, Mrs. Israel, once gave me a "Needs Improvement" in following directions, she was wrong. I followed them too well. I became the sorcerer's apprentice of obedience.

It was now three o'clock and the thought of returning to the ostentation of the women's store was unappealing, even for research purposes. Well, what about that fifth floor? If all else failed, I could look at shoes.

We went back. I saw the taupe suede Birkenstocks and suddenly had to have them. Reverse chic, I know, but also relentlessly ugly and comfortable. Not that I usually yearn to buy something ugly, but this shopping trip was pushing my buttons—the CHEAP button, the I DON'T DESERVE button—and I was tired of both. I'd already indulged in the manicure, my fingernails sparkling idiotically in the fluorescent light, giving me no satisfaction at all. And these shoes were affordable, practical and almost indestructible. I craved them.

While I tried them on, the salesman insisted on showing me Birkenstocks for evening. They were gold with rhinestone buckles and sold for $298. A customer bought two pairs last week, he said, to wear as slippers.

Okay, that was enough. This day's entertainment had officially drawn to a close. I would peruse my catalogues all by myself and hope for the best.

Outside on Fifth Avenue, the sun was still shining. Phoebe gave me a kiss and went off happily to Ann Taylor. Her shopping day was young. I looked for a cab halfheartedly. I knew that this was the moment I should turn around, charge back upstairs and buy the Calvin Klein sweater, proving to myself that I was worth it, that I could break all the dumb patterns of behavior that have their roots in rotten places and that if I went ahead and bought it and got ketchup on the damn thing the world wouldn't come to an end.

A cab pulled up to the curb. I went to the office.

chapter three

Behind Bars

My catalogue shopping went just fine, and I was able, with the help mostly of J.Crew, to rejoin the human race in time for summer. I'd worry about the sweaters later. Of course, there was still the issue of bathing suits. Is there anything worse? The idea of buying one through the mail is always more appealing than standing in a dressing room where the door doesn't quite close and a snooping saleslady is all too eager to help adjust the top. I prefer to be humiliated in the privacy of my own home.

Three. I own three bathing suits, and two are from college. Buying bathing suits was always traumatic. First of all, Mom insisted that when we tried one on we keep our underwear on. It wasn't sanitary otherwise. So there I'd be, hoping that somehow, when I took off my underwear, the bottoms might suddenly fit like a dream. Surprise! They never did.

As I recall, my very first bikini was a fetching number in pink with a daisy print. I was thirteen at the time, and quite comfortable in it, hanging out with my friends at camp during swim instruction. That is, until I saw the two eighteen-year-old male instructors pointing at us and laughing. Because there we were, a group of giggling girls with morphing bodies who were still sitting on the dock like children, legs splayed any which way, with no idea that our brand-new pubic hair was showing. Who knew from a bikini wax? I was beyond mortified, we all were, and I never forgave them. Even years later when I actually dated one of them, if you can believe it, I sat across the dinner table and told myself it was finally time to put childish things behind me and stop holding a grudge. So, I finished my dessert and never saw him again.

This was also the age when tits began, though everyone else's seemed to start first. By eighth grade I was still flat as a pancake and Dorinda Haskel used to come to my house with her clinging shirts and I thought she was the equivalent of Jayne Mansfield until she had left and Mom would say, "Oh, I saw Dorinda here, admiring her cupcakes in the mirror." Well, when you've still got cookies, cupcakes are something to aspire to.

As was Mom, of course. Where else do you learn body image? I was in ninth grade before my cupcakes had finally risen, but my hips were beating them out in the competition for space. And I cried, huge hurricanes of tears, because Susan Edbril had cupcakes *and* a body like an iodine bottle. She was perfect. Mom tried to be comforting.

"You have good hips for childbearing," she offered. Childbearing? Who gave a shit about that? I wanted to be a cheerleader, not a child-bearer. And it only made matters worse to go shopping with Susan, as I used to at Loehmann's. There we would be in that big communal dressing room, me crying about my hips and Susan with her perfect body, crying too. Why? Because she was so skinny, her ribs stuck out. I could kill her just thinking about it.

When it came to teenage summers on the beach, I suffered, though

I must say that for all my weeping, my appetite was never diminished one iota for the roast-beef hero sandwiches we brought along with us. Somehow, when I was hungry, there was no connection between what I put in my mouth and what I saw in the mirror. But the summer I was sixteen, I was saved. Greg was turning thirteen, and my parents decided to have his bar mitzvah in Israel, which spared me the perpetual view of Susan's string bikini. Once we got to the King David Hotel in Jerusalem and I ventured nervously toward the pool, I saw a collection of bodies I could not believe. Apparently no one there had ever read *Seventeen*. Fat, scarred, sagging, even nine months pregnant, and each one strutting like Farrah Fawcett. Maybe I wasn't so bad after all, I reassured myself, a notion that lasted until the minute I got home.

That summer we stayed in Israel the whole time instead of following our usual custom of going to sleepover camp, then renting a house in the Hamptons. And I was just as glad to skip it. The only drawback to the experience was that the food in Israel was truly disgusting, starting with the tomatoes and cucumbers they served for breakfast. I spent eight weeks teen-touring and dreaming about pizza.

But first, the bar mitzvah. While so many other things over there were totally different from home, when it came to religion, the approach was dishearteningly similar. An Orthodox temple is an Orthodox temple, it would seem, no matter where it is. And on the great day there we were, me, Mom and Phoebe crammed upstairs behind screens, with Mom practically falling over the side in her efforts to see her eldest son become a man.

She ultimately succeeded, as I recall, though every time I tried, I could never see Greg, blocked by the hordes of men in my way. But this was how my father wanted it, and in our house religion was a nonnegotiable. Even though Mom had been raised in a Jewish household, her family were bona fide heathens compared to Dad's. Not only did they not keep kosher (Campbell's Soup, call the cops!) but they actually skipped pages in the Haggadah during the seder. *Oy gevalt!*

In Dad's family, not only was every page, nay, every paragraph, read, so were the italics inside the brackets. They could also tell you the exact time the sun went down and when the Sabbath candles should be lit. And they never turned on an electric light or the television or radio on Yom Kippur. But, over the years of my parents' marriage, Mom put her dainty foot down more than a few times and tiny insurrections eventually occurred.

Like, finally, we were allowed to order in pizza, as long as it didn't have sausage or pepperoni on it and as long as we ate it in the garage on paper plates. Same with Chinese as long as there was no pork, and we could eat that too, in the garage with plastic forks. There's a gourmet dining experience for you. Nothing like carbon monoxide fumes to really bring out the nuance of a lobster Cantonese. (When you're kosher you're not supposed to eat pork or shellfish, but don't even try to figure out how my father distinguished between the two. The minute he left the house, lobster was his first priority.)

I thought Mom must have lost her mind to marry into this regimented existence and have to endure its litany of don'ts. And although I wanted to grow up to be like her in every way, this was not one of them. She did prevail, though, when it came to sitting separately on the High Holidays. Since this was when she had planned her appearances, she wanted the family together. So in addition to belonging to an Orthodox synagogue, we also belonged to a Conservative synagogue, where the girls were allowed to sit with the boys. At this place the bigger issue was whose family sat up front and who had the cheap seats.

The seating issue was symbolic of the rift we all seemed to have with being Jewish, even Dad. Sometimes we were Orthodox and sometimes we weren't. The rules were copious, but each one seemed made to be broken. Suburbs or shtetl? It depended on the day.

My own feeling about the Orthodox synagogue (Rabbi Grauer notwithstanding) was that it was not for me. In Hebrew school, I learned every prayer faster and better than any boy in the class, but, unlike them, I was not allowed to participate in the service. And though the synagogue we belong to keeps everyone on the ground floor, the upstairs pen having been abolished, I still don't like it. The men sit in the middle, facing God. The women sit on the sides, facing the men. Talk about progress.

I liked the Conservative temple better, if only because the rabbi there was a hoot. One night, several members of the congregation caught him at a restaurant called the Clam Box scarfing a lobster, not to mention the fact that in his spare time he was boffing the president of the sisterhood. There's some entertainment value for your membership fee.

For the kids in our family, Jewish observance never took a summer holiday, but continued straight through Camp Cejwin in Port Jervis, New York. It was kosher, of course, and run by B'nai B'rith. They didn't just have two sets of dishes for milk and meat, they had two separate kitchens for milk and meat. Very hard core.

Religion aside, I loved that camp, which closed in 1992 and was included in a recent exhibition about summer camps at the Jewish Museum in New York. I couldn't bring myself to see it there, enshrined as an artifact of twentieth-century Jewish life. Too depressing. It was depressing enough that after years at Cejwin perfecting my Israeli folk dancing, I went to Israel and found that no one my age knew how to folk dance, although they could take apart an Uzi in less than three minutes. Well, I thought that was pretty cool and informed my parents that I would be joining the Israeli army (girls allowed!) as soon as possible. In turn, they informed me that they were confiscating my passport and I was grounded for life. Uzi not included.

Something we learned in camp, as we learned at home, was *tzeda-kah*, which means charity. At the end of the summer we were given a list of potential worthy causes that we were to designate as recipients of the money we donated. I was the problem child of the bunk because instead of voting for Hadassah or the Jewish National Fund, I was pushing the American Cancer Society, which could help everyone, not just Jews. "No one helps the Jews except the Jews," I could hear both parents' voices echo in my head, but I didn't like being a Jew first and a person second. So our bunk made two contributions.

What I really loved best about Camp Cejwin (be still, my heart) was Ricky Plotkin. He was from Bayside, Queens, and he looked like a combination of Paul McCartney and Al Pacino in *Serpico*. He was a terrific kisser and he also gave a world-class hickey. I would happily pray before and after breakfast, lunch and dinner, as we did, to go to a social with Ricky Plotkin. I also became a master at leading raids from the girls' side (at the top of the mountain) to the boys' side at the bottom, without ever getting caught. And prayer had nothing to do with it.

Each year when camp ended, I was distraught. And thoroughly unmoved by the brightly written letters Mom would start sending at the beginning of August. We have the most wonderful plans, she would say, to go to the Hamptons when you come home from camp. We are going to rent a house out there for ten days and go to the beach and eat lobster and have a real rest before school starts again.

Of course, she was the one who wanted the rest before her school started again. I, who led raids at 3:00 A.M., had no interest in resting. I was not only rendezvousing with an expert fifteen-year-old make-out artist, I was a genuine revolutionary. I was finally breaking out of the girls' section up top and invading the boys' territory down below, and though I still wasn't reading from the Torah, I loved it.

Who wanted to go home and follow rules? Or even worse, go

someplace where I had no friends, no boyfriend and no hickeys, and be with my parents, who had nothing else to pay attention to except their children? A punishment worse than death.

But in spite of what I wanted, after the last weepy night of camp ended, we would arrive home and the minute I got there I would get on the phone and call everyone I could, and I wasn't there an hour before Dad started to yell and Mom looked woebegone and wondered aloud if I wouldn't like to spend any time with her at all.

And after a day or two of laundry and repacking, there we would be, at some house in the Hamptons that didn't smell like our house and didn't look like our house, and none of us seemed too happy about it. But Mom played her trump card. In these houses, we didn't have to be kosher. They weren't ours. We could go to the supermarket and buy every godforsaken thing we saw in commercials, eat it for lunch and have a ball.

Well, this had possibilities. Most of the time we were stuck heating up cans of Hebrew National Braised Beef and Rice. I didn't know one other kid who ever ate that. So we picked out Swanson fried chicken TV dinners and SpaghettiOs, bore them triumphantly back to the stranger's kitchen and practically gagged. But it looked so good on television, we cried, while my parents smirked big I-told-you-so's. This adventure over, I wanted to go back to camp again.

Then it would be forever until dinner (we went out every night, since, after all, Mom was on vacation too), and we invariably ended up someplace with long tables, draft beer and lobsters. My mother eats a lobster like a cutter handles a diamond. Every movement is excruciatingly deliberate, every shred of meat accounted for, every shard of shell cleaned. She can make one and a half pounds of lobster last for hours. And while we were all hanging around waiting for her to finish the damn roe, which she saved for last, wondering how much of *Love, American Style* we were going to miss, someone would play a song on the jukebox and I would yearn again for Ricky Plotkin, who, no doubt, was yearning double for me. And I would think, "Mommy just doesn't understand how I feel," sitting here dissecting this stupid lobster when all I want to do is go back to camp. And when I would say this to her accusatorially, tears trembling in my eyes at such terrible insensitivity, she would look at me as if I had lost my mind.

"Camp is over," she would say, wielding her cracker. "What are you going to go back to? Everyone else went home too." And her irrefutable logic would choke me with frustration, since I actually had no choice but to sit and watch her eat everything but the feelers at exactly the pace that pleased her.

"Do you remember how you would do that?" I demanded of her years later as we drove to the Hamptons together. It was a month or two after my Bergdorf trip and fresh adventures beckoned. We were going to spend a night together at the new Bridgehampton Motel, but at the moment our present activity was not my immediate concern. "Do you remember?" I pressed, my anger renewed. "How you would eat that damned thing forever?"

"Yes," she said calmly. "And I still do."

Undeterred by my bad Hamptons attitude, Mom's fascination with the area had progressed unabated, like that of most people in New York. She was willing to brave the killer traffic to drive all the way through Long Island to its easternmost part, continuing to spend two weeks every summer in a rented apartment there with Dad, long after the rest of us jumped ship. Sitting on the beach has always bored me (bathing-suit dramas aside) but she loves it. And she manages to avoid all the social nonsense out there, the behavior which makes me so sick that I never go if I can help it. Those endless cocktail parties where you can see the same people from the city you can't stand during the week, only now you can see their elbows, armpits, hammertoes and varicose veins. Unless of course it's a really fancy party, and then you can watch the women wearing stockings in the middle of July, mincing across the lawns, their high heels sinking into the grass, leaving eternal stains. Actually, that part is always fun.

But those who treasure the Hamptons and can't afford to own property there usually find themselves sunk as serious social climbers. There's no place acceptable to stay long-term, and most houseguests are only slotted one weekend per summer, two at most, at someone's cherished abode. When the Bridgehampton Motel opened under the ownership of Alexis Stewart, the twenty-five-year-old daughter of Martha Stewart, the perky home-entertaining author, climbers sighed with relief, eager to pay the whopping tariff of $245 per night. And to up the ante, there are only ten rooms. When I called to book one—on assignment, of course—Saturday nights were already gone, so we opted for a Thursday night instead, arriving about noon. We found a standard flat-roofed strip of a building with a big gravel parking lot bordered by hydrangeas. It looked like Iowa.

We requested a smoking room, even though smoking has become the cooties of the nineties, and were assigned Room 10, all the way at the end, next to the laundry. The upside of Room 10 was that it was farthest from the highway. The downside was that the washing machine began at sunrise.

From the look of the place I ventured a guess that Alexis Stewart had also had her fill of the Hamptons, or at least the Hamptons of her mother's generation. Her motel was a battle cry against cabbage roses, throw pillows and hooked rugs. It was no place like home. The windows' plain white shades matched the bare white walls. There was one chair near the television, but, as Mom pointed out, no table for a book, a drink or the sole ashtray in this smoking room.

"Not very welcoming," she said, shaking her head. To smoke simultaneously we'd have to sit next to each other on the bed. The view from the front window was of the parking lot; from the rear, the generator. The bathroom was tiny (more white) with a toilet and shower stall. One gleam of color came from the gold cover of a Gideon Bible. Ms. Stewart apparently took "Lead us not into temptation" very much to heart.

Mom and I sat side by side, sharing the ashtray, while I continued to vent my rediscovered adolescent frustration over camp and the lobsters. She was as sympathetic now as she was then.

"That's the way it goes," she said briskly.

"That's it? The scars of my childhood revealed and all I get is 'that's the way it goes'?"

"Sorry, sweetheart. How about a tuna-fish sandwich?"

Well, if that was all she was offering, I was going to take it. Tuna-fish sandwiches are our family's madeleines, and the recipe for the filling is as secret as parental sex. She did write it down for me once, but I'm sorry to say the result was not the same. I did a taste test, mine on one plate, hers on the other and gave them to Simon, my younger stepson, who, upon meeting my mother, became an instant tuna-fish disciple. In less than three seconds he identified hers, and very politely handed the other plate back.

We sat outside, but there wasn't much to see, except Mom unwrapping the sandwiches. I hope she owns stock in Reynolds Wrap. She doesn't wrap something just once in aluminum foil. She wrapes it at least twice, then in plastic and sometimes she'll even put a rubber band around it.

Our car was the only one in the lot. I focused on the large tree instead.

"The apples smell great," I said.

"I don't smell a thing," Mom said.

I pulled a bough close to my face. Nothing. Then I realized it was the organic apple juice she had taken from the minibar.

Mom was vastly unimpressed by the motel. She is the person who taught me always to be vastly unimpressed by pretense, and the fact that we were sitting three yards from a parking lot looking at a row of identical doors and paying almost $300 for the privilege rankled her. But the difference between us is that while I complain volubly when dissatisfied, Mom is more tactful, reserved. Women of her generation learned that lesson early: to swallow bad feelings and look on the bright side. They called it good manners. A concept, much to her chagrin, I had no use for. Why not come right out and say what you think?

She'd sigh and shake her head at me disapprovingly, her brash daughter with the big mouth. Though every once in a while, to her everlasting credit, Mom gives way to a display of will and pique that makes me look like an amateur.

Last year, for instance, when we were at Rosh Hashanah services. Not in the Conservative synagogue, where my father decided he was infinitely less entertained by the rabbi's shenanigans than I was, but at the Orthodox synagogue, where propriety, and Rabbi Grauer, reigned. To meet the state requirements as a nonprofit institution, the synagogue had installed a ramp for handicapped access and in doing so had to raise the floor. In turn, to be in accordance with the rules about these things, they also had to raise the separation between the men and women, so they installed some horizontal bars above the wooden partitions that already separated them.

Well, Mom can nod and smile with the best of them, but to sit behind bars was another story.

"I can't believe this," she gasped, as we sat down. She was quiet for a while, in her tight-mouth mode. Then, in the middle of the service, she just grabbed hold with two hands and started shaking the bars as if she were a prisoner. I burst out laughing. Some of the old ladies looked on, horrified, but I couldn't stop. These lapses in Mom's well-mannered façade are truly my inspiration. My father pretended not to notice, or maybe he really didn't, shunted off to the side as we were. In any case, he felt the same way about it as we did. But when I started laughing, so did Phoebe, and almost in spite of herself so did Mom, and later in the day I heard a few women talk about forming a committee to see if they could do something about removing those bars. She's a revolutionary herself, that mother of mine, when every once in a while, even for her, the rules become ridiculous.

As for the Bridgehampton Motel, she had quickly decided that she had no use for this place, hyped in all the papers, but she would never knock it. Of course, if she did, her stomach might feel better. But that is not her way.

I remember when we moved to Scarsdale, a ritzy suburb of New York, famous for its snobs. I was twelve at the time, and the very first night, my father's business partner, who also lived there, invited our family for dinner. We arrived bedraggled after a day of moving, the kids all cranky and scared about a new school, Mom in pants, still slightly dusty and completely spent. This man's wife, who didn't work and spent great amounts of time in Maine chasing crafts, greeted us in a hostess skirt, down to the floor, which was so rotten to my mother, who hadn't had a moment even to locate her good clothes, much less change into them. When we sat down to dinner the maid served from the left and cleared from the right and I was mightily impressed, even though I saw our hostess take sharp note that none of us kids were used to being served and didn't know when it was our turn to pick up the big fork and spoon and chance the trip from platter to plate.

My mother saw all of this too, but her behavior remained impeccable. I would have gladly strangled this woman, with her artfully woven placemats indigenous to a souvenir shop in Kennebunkport. But Mom was gracious and warm and said how grateful she was that her family was being fed on such a hectic day, and on and on. As if we couldn't have just eaten out. Years later, when I had collected a boyfriend whose father was so enamored of his Jaguar sedan that he would fill the water tank only with Perrier, she kept her mouth pressed shut, but I'll never forget her Oh-Alex-honestly! expression. She was fearing for her gene pool.

Two sandwiches later, we went back to our room, where we quickly realized that being there made us want to leave. Maybe that's the difference between a hotel and a motel. We went to the beach for a while, and then we shopped. I bought a pasta bowl at Kitchen Classics in Bridgehampton, and Mom bought wooden trivets to put underneath her plants. It is my mother's secret fantasy to be a florist. Give her a sickly African violet, and she'll hand you back six sturdy ones. Give me a cactus, it'll be dead in a week. This, she says, is because I have no patience. If I water a plant and it doesn't grow or blossom by the time the can is empty, I feel I've done a bad job and lose interest. And then I give it to her.

We drove into East Hampton and walked around, and because we hadn't eaten in at least two hours, got ice-cream cones and sat on a bench on the main street. We were in the shade and there weren't too many people around and a wonderful feeling of calm came to me that never seems to happen on the beach with the sun in my eyes and someone else's radio in my ear.

"Look at that store," Mom said, amazed, pointing across the street. "They sell only white clothes."

Then I pointed out the stationery store near it and wondered if they still sold individual gift bags for wine, the way they used to. "You know, in packages," I said, "not separate and so expensive."

And we talked about the way no one seemed to have those anymore and about how we would both just go crazy working in a place that was all white with no color. And as we finished our cones I slid my hand into hers and she held it. She leaned over and kissed my cheek and I kissed hers in turn, and we sat on the bench saying nothing for a long time. Our hands are the same size and it almost felt as if I had clasped my own, though I rarely do that except in anxiety and this was peace.

And I thought of all the plans we make in our lives to get together and go out to dinner and see shows and have a good time, and here we are, on a bench in East Hampton, where all we're doing is avoiding our motel room and we've found absolute communion. Here on this bench now, in summer, we have no age. I am five and fifteen and thirty-five and this is my mom here next to me as she has always been. Our hands, still a little slippery from the suntan lotion, held firm.

Finally, finally, we faced the inevitable. We bought a bottle of Maker's Mark bourbon and returned to discover the motel's A+ feature. With a water pressure unknown to most prewar Manhattan apartments, this shower bordered on the spiritual. The high came to a premature end upon discovering that the hair dryer affixed to the wall did not work. Never fear. Mom had one in her Sportsac, whose previous owner was apparently Mary Poppins.

My mother actually does not travel a great deal, but from her preparation you'd never know it. Her travel bag is the best I've ever seen, with little bottles of every brand she uses and an endless supply of tissues, bobby pins, safety pins, anything you'd need in a pinch. All the years I've known her she has kept that bag packed and ready on the floor of her closet, even when months would go by without her using it.

I wonder about that now. I remember when I first moved into my new apartment with Frank, we had only been living there a few days and had an argument. And I thought, screw it, I'm out of here, I'll talk to him about it later. And as I was getting my purse to leave, I had to stop and wonder where exactly it was I was going. I lived there now. I didn't have my own place anymore. What an airless moment that was.

I wonder about everywhere else Mom might have wished to be instead of standing at the counter making hamburger patties, scrubbing the broiler, marking her papers at the dinner table, waking up in the middle of the night to whichever plaintive call of "Mommy!" had floated to her bedside. That bag meant something to her. Just having it there, packed and ready, might have been enough. She could leave if she wanted to. But she stayed. Because she wanted to. Even if it felt like she had to.

It was time for dinner. Our appetite for the new, trendy and fabulous had been exhausted by the room, so we opted for the Lobster Roll in Amagansett, better known as Lunch. Perhaps taking pity on me retroactively, Mom did not order a lobster. We both had lobster rolls, french fries and beer. I ate like a maniac, which I usually do when I'm with Mom. I somehow think I'm still growing.

Back at the motel, the night clerk cautioned that "Alexis is very strict about checkout time," which was noon. No problem. When the newspapers hit the front door like a bomb the next morning, it was all of 6:30. Plenty of time left.

I went to the office at exactly noon, trying to ignore the maid pacing outside the door. She must have had a hot lunch date. Outside the office was Alexis Stewart, tall and blonde with five miles of leg, in Lycra shorts and a skintight T-shirt, being photographed.

As the photo session moved to one of the unoccupied guest rooms, the clerk behind the desk was breaking into a sweat because the computer would not print my bill. I waited while she punched the keyboard over and over.

Ms. Stewart, hastily summoned from her promotional duties, examined it. "You need to press the button that says 'on-line,'" she told the wilted clerk, annoyed. She turned briefly in my direction. "Sorry," she said, looking at nothing in particular. No time for conversation. Publicity awaited.

With the bill finally in my bag, I couldn't help feeling ripped off. When we got back to my apartment Phoebe came over and she and Frank admired my new pasta bowl before he left for a business dinner.

We poured some bourbon all around, ordered some sushi to be delivered and the three of us climbed into my bed to watch the sun set.

"Tell me about the motel," Phoebe urged, convinced she had missed the experience of a lifetime. "Was it cool?"

"I don't know," I yawned. "Let Mommy tell you."

Mom smiled. "Well," she said, "it had a terrific shower."

Phoebe looked blank. "Yeah. And?" she said.

"Mommy didn't like it, can't you tell?" I asked. Then the phone rang. And as soon as I wasn't listening, Mom started to tell her all the things she didn't like, but in a very low voice, like maybe I wouldn't hear.

"Mom, I don't care if you didn't like it," I said after hanging up. "I didn't like it either. Just because I asked you to come there with me doesn't mean it had to be perfect."

"I know that," she said and made a funny face, and snuggled with Phoebe on my pillows because she hates confrontation no matter how minor, and she loves spending time with her girls, as she puts it, so she didn't want to criticize the experience in any way.

And I had to admit to myself then that of course I had wanted her to love it. I want her to love everything I do, everything I think, everything I say. She's my mom. Though as I get older the balance is starting to shift a little, and I find I want her to be more like me. Outspoken, tougher. So that I'll feel better that I'm not like her. Even though I thought I would be. Counted on it, in fact. It scares me a little to know this, because I automatically feel I'm doing something wrong. Isn't imitation the sincerest form of flattery? With mothers it goes even further. It's the sincerest form of justification. Of their lives.

I've noticed recently that when I see myself unexpectedly in the bathroom mirror, sometimes I see Mom there, looking back at me.

Usually it's when I'm tired. But it makes me glad. It makes me feel that I have company. She's in there, somehow. And then I catch myself. Isn't separation supposed to have happened when I was about three? I guess I'm only a few decades late. It just seems to me, ultimately, a disloyal process. No, thank you, actually I'd rather not grow up to be just like you, after all. My mistake. Pass the sugar?

The three of us stayed on my bed for a long time and talked. And even though it was only July, we planned the menu for Thanksgiving, which is a really big deal in our family, when everyone comes to our house, both my father's sisters and my uncle and cousins, and now, the kids.

You might not be surprised to hear that Thanksgiving is my favorite holiday. After all, it's secular. And even though we always have potato kugel with the turkey, and my father can't quite restrain himself from donning a yarmulke to bless something, we aren't actually supposed to do anything religious. And I love it. For one night, we're American first, or as American as we're going to get living in New York.

Of course there's a ritual on Thanksgiving at our house, the same way everyone has a ritual. The first thing that happens is that Mom wakes up. Until that moment, nothing's going on. But once she plugs in her Salton hot trays, watch out. There's not a spare inch of kitchen left.

She roasts the turkey and makes a brisket. Both. "You don't eat properly," she chides us in our apartments, looking suspiciously at bowls of tofu or brown rice. In her house we look at the brisket and ask, "This is properly, Mom? This is a heart attack."

"This is iron," she says without missing a beat. "It gives you energy." Which comes in handy for conversations like this.

She also makes too many side dishes, but no matter how many there are, there is also a dish of green and black olives that appears somewhere on the table. What exactly went on in the fifties that caused this olive fixation? I look through some of her old cookbooks and see olives stuffed with cream cheese, processed into hams and floating in martinis. It seems to be the tabletop equivalent of "a woman isn't dressed without her hat and gloves."

I might add that I've never seen anyone eat these olives until maybe Sunday of Thanksgiving weekend, when there's nothing else left. The same dish has been pushed all the way to the back of the refrigerator, covered in Saran Wrap, onto which, by then, something has dripped. By the time you've wiped it off and unwrapped it and noticed that the pitted black kind have started to shrivel down one side, you're completely sorry you did.

On Thanksgiving Day itself, everyone arrives by four. There's a fire in the fireplace and a football game is on television, but I never know who's playing. I contribute the same dish every year, canned pears mashed into canned cranberry sauce, a recipe I learned in tenth grade from the kind of girl who read *Good Housekeeping* before her time. (It actually tastes much better than it sounds.) Mom wears an apron over a silk dress and goes rushing around the house replenishing tables of hors d'oeuvres that could easily pass for a buffet lunch. Tuna fish (but of course), crackers, chopped liver, salami, knishes, cocktail franks.

A video camera has appeared recently, but no one seems to know how to use it. They're still working on the Instamatic. "Did the flash go off?" has been as constant a question at these dinners as "White meat or dark?" one of life's never-ending mysteries. During drinks there is usually one political discussion ("You voted for WHO?"), one theater discussion in honor of my husband, once the *Times* drama critic ("What's the season like, Frank?") and one vacation discussion ("We followed the tour bus in our car and didn't have to pay!"). Six o'clock means dinner.

Here's where I start to jump up and down from the table, first helping Mom to serve, then clearing plates, while Phoebe, cleverly seated on the side of the table farthest from the kitchen, enjoys the view. "Hey, Cinderella," she'll cackle. Then my Aunt Marcia, who brings the potato kugel, tells a few jokes, which are always funny, but which inspire everyone else to tell jokes that aren't. Then it's dessert and a huge array appears, and everyone talks about how delicious they all are and I'm sure they're right, but I ran out of room after the tuna fish and slipped my brisket to Frank while Mom was distracted and I'll just have tea, thanks.

And in the kitchen is Mom, now making her care packages for everyone to take home. She is a vision of flying arms, Reynolds Wrap and Tupperware. Not to mention rubber bands. By this point, I've bummed one of her cigarettes to steel myself for negotiations with the kids, who want to stay long enough to watch their favorite TV programs while all the while Frank is signaling for help in escaping yet one more roundtable on Morris Carnovsky's interpretation of Lear. And earlier in the meal, probably at the point when ten dishes of food are being passed, someone says remember so-and-so? Well, he dropped dead last week, and as they supply all the gory details of how, Greg turns to me and says, "Woody Allen, or what?" and I say, "Jew eat?" and since that's what we do every year, no one pays us any mind at all.

And then we finally go home and unpack the care packages and after swearing I would never eat again, I'm watching David Letterman in the kitchen while standing at the counter, loading the microwave and unloading it into my mouth. "Sit down like a person," I can hear my mother say. And so I call her, and she's finally out of the kitchen, watching a *Murphy Brown* rerun, not Letterman, and I tell her what I'm eating and where and she says, "Why don't you take out a plate and sit down?"

Now that my worldview has been confirmed, it dawns on me to ask

how she is and the very surprising answer is, "Tired." I never like to
think of my mother as tired. Tired is for mortals, not mothers. Though,
when I was growing up, she would say to me more often than I care to
remember: "It's time for you to go to bed now. *I'm* tired."

It used to be that the day after Thanksgiving, Mom, Phoebe and I
would go shopping, braving the crowds, but we've stopped that since
I've been married and I can't say I miss it. What I do miss is coming
home afterward and Mom making turkey hash and feeling the luxury
of a long weekend wrap around me, convinced that Sunday night is
years away. And when it finally does come and the reality of Monday
and all its horrors looms, what's left to comfort you? Olives.

Our holiday menu planned, we hauled ourselves out of my bed and
ate our sushi. And when Mom and Phoebe left that night I didn't see
them again for weeks, between various vacation schedules, until Rosh
Hashanah, after which we settled down to wait for Thanksgiving.

In the meantime, I had another assignment, a small Irish hotel
called the Fitzpatrick Manhattan. Like a reflex, I asked Mom to come,
even though I was feeling tired of escaping *à deux*. I was in a cranky
mode, fed up for no good reason with everything—job, kids, Frank,
Mom. So? She wasn't asking to come with me. Why was I offering?
Because I am the best daughter in the world, and don't you forget it. I
certainly couldn't.

Once Phoebe heard about our plans, she wailed again.

"When do I get to stay over?" she demanded.

"Never," I said calmly. "But you can do the rest with us."

I heard something like "big deal" muttered on the other end of the
phone, quickly replaced by a game and cheery, "Okay."

What was I proving here? That Mommy loved me more because
I had a hotel room and she didn't? Actually, yes, that was it, exactly.
What a gal.

We had reserved a suite because the weekend rate was such a bargain. It was called the Robinson Suite, as in Mary, president of Ireland. A photograph of her hung in the living room, where I looked at it and felt immediately guilty. Mary Robinson probably never wanted to escape from life, or her mother, or her sister, and behaved perfectly in all situations. Which is why she's president of a country and I'm here taking notes on the floral print bedspread on the bed where I wouldn't even let my sister sneak in for one night. Not because I'm such a great daughter—let the truth be told—but because I need my mother to pay total attention only to me. And instead of enjoying it, I resent it. Now, that makes perfect sense.

We went downstairs for tea at Fitzer's, a bar and restaurant connected to the hotel, and talked about how much better we liked this place than the Bridgehampton Motel. They brought us sandwiches, chicken, ham and Irish smoked salmon. Mom ate the ham. Whenever we ate out as kids, it was Mom who got BLTs, chewing past my father's glare. He didn't dare say anything though, considering his lobster exploits, but he definitely did not approve. I still don't eat ham, unless it's called prosciutto. Because then it isn't ham.

Phoebe came in from the gallery to join us and complained for a good ten minutes about her day. Then, just to keep the spirit of the thing going, I did too. Mom didn't, of course. She nodded sympathetically and told us both to "think positively." Which is what she always says.

We went back to the suite and fell straight into bed.

My throat hurt. Mom gave me Aspergum. My throat stopped hurting. How does that work, exactly? Is my child's wish to be taken care of so powerful that my brain just guarantees I respond? Or is it something more base than that? Just knowing by smell or pulse somehow that this is my mother, so all is well? I can't tell. I think it's like hypnosis, because when I'm with Mom and she's taking care of me, it's like someone intoning, "You're getting sleepy." And then it's no longer my problem that the window leaked or my check to American Express got lost in the mail. There's a layer between me and the elements of the outside world that's impenetrable. Mommy. No wonder I fight so hard for her.

Inspired by the sight of the wet bar, we held a brief caucus on the merits of trying to assemble an impromptu "Here's to you, Mrs. Robinson" cocktail party. But it was already 7:30, so who would come?

Actually, as far as parties go, none of us is too terrific at them. When I was fourteen, I wanted a birthday party, but Mom saw me coming. When I turned thirteen, she had gone out and bought me a snappy ensemble from Saks of wool pants, silk blouse and a knit vest that I wouldn't be caught dead in. Everyone else in my grade was wearing bell-bottom jeans and man-tailored shirts. I pitched an absolute fit and she pitched one back about my being an ungrateful child. So when I turned fourteen, instead of a party, she gave me a (paperback!) copy of *Between Parent and Child* and defrosted a Pepperidge Farm cake instead of getting one from the bakery with the pink buttercream roses I loved.

Besides the fact that it was frozen, this cake's other distinguishing feature was that it was yellow, with chocolate icing and chocolate filling. That's fine, but that was the flavor Phoebe likes. Sometimes Mom would get me all chocolate, which is what she likes, and one year, in a burst of goodwill, Dad bought me a birthday cake that was strawberry shortcake, his favorite. My own favorite was yellow with raspberry filling and white frosting, and I couldn't get one for love or money. No one could remember. Mom finally learned, but it's useless to point out now that my taste has changed and I'd like something else. I would be fifty before I got it.

As for my parents' anniversaries, of course, all my presents have been perfect. I remember when I was still fourteen (I think I was fourteen for about fourteen years) I saved my money in the tissue box I used as a bank and sent my parents to see *Butterflies Are Free* on Broadway. They liked going to the theater, though never as much as I did, and I really should admit, after all my cake accusations, that I wish I had gone to see this show, not them. But I figured that because the story was about people from Scarsdale, they would like it.

They came home looking tired and thoroughly untransported, which I couldn't imagine after going to the theater. Obviously Mom had told Dad not to say anything bad about it and so he didn't, but she didn't say much either, except that she had appreciated my sending them. It just didn't seem possible that any one of us could make the others happy.

It was 8:00 now, so we decided to scrap the party idea and went to the Landmark Tavern instead, to be in keeping with our Irish theme. After some whiskey and a basket of freshly baked Irish soda bread we were revived. Or at least I was. Mom and Phoebe started having a fight, but I could barely follow it. They fight so differently with each other than I do with Mom—I yell and she listens. Then she says something reasonable and I calm down and that's it.

With Mom and Phoebe, Mom behaves more like she did with Grandma, whom Phoebe resembles in more ways than perhaps Mom would like. They speak to each other quietly, getting in their little digs and then Mom produces a tight mouth and Phoebe starts to freak, but they both keep up the pretense that nothing untoward is happening. At the moment, the issue seemed to be Mom's stomach, which Phoebe had more or less appropriated as a cause since they both started seeing the same nutritionist. Phoebe's stomach tends to react to the world the same way Mom's does, and since Mom was eating shepherd's pie for dinner, which had a number of no-no ingredients, she took some pill or other to aid her digestion and Phoebe immediately wanted to know what it was. And then Mom, as she sometimes does, got into this privacy kick, like "What business is it of yours what I'm taking?" even though they both see the same doctor and she'd told her everything else so far. She just decides to switch her signals midstream and snap, snap, quick on the uptake, we're supposed to follow along.

She was probably feeling the same way I had about needing escape. Is there any privacy after you become a wife? Or a parent? Not really. Kids are a constant audience and you are the star of their show. They are absolutely riveted by you, but sooner or later everyone needs down time. Especially now, I could see, so I got the check while Phoebe did the obligatory I-don't-want-to-go-home, even though they were still fighting, but we dropped her off at her apartment anyway and returned to the Fitzpatrick.

I got into my nightgown (a decent one this time) and Mom settled in with the remote, ready to watch *Murphy Brown*.

"Don't you want to watch Letterman?" I asked.

"No, I don't like him. I don't think he's funny."

"Really? Didn't you see when he had that guy shot out of the cannon?"

"Exactly. What's funny?"

So she went into the living room to watch *Murphy Brown* and *Designing Women* and I lay in bed watching Letterman and missing Frank. I felt lonely, not only for him, but also for Mom. I used to like everything she liked. Or maybe I just thought I did. When I stopped to think about it, it seemed that we hadn't actually learned anything about each other in years. I mean, we paid closer attention to *things*, like what to buy for a gift, but even though my mother knows every fact of my life, as I do of hers, neither of us seems able to reach out and wrap a hand around that jumble of aches and wishes the other wakes up with. And because I consider us to be close, I can't help but find that odd.

A few months after I got married, I asked her to spend a Sunday with me at the New York Botanical Garden. I wanted to talk to her about marriage, ask her whether the things I was feeling were right.

Meaning, I guess, that I was feeling what she had felt. And there we were walking through roomfuls of ferns and I looked at her face, calm and peaceful, and my mouth would not open. And I thought, "Mommy, look at me, answer the questions I want to ask, see into my soul and understand it all for me and with me and let me know everything will be all right." But she didn't. And I said nothing. I couldn't. Because I realized there was a new split between us. She couldn't be married with me.

When her TV programs were finished, she came back to the bedroom and kissed me good night. Her cheek was so soft. When my brother Emmett was a little boy he kissed me once and shook his head disapprovingly. "Mommy's cheek is better," he said. "Yours is too springy. Mommy's cheek sinks all the way in." It still does. And I fell into a dead sleep, in spite of the fact that she left the bathroom light on again.

We slept until ten, and stayed in the room reading the paper and Mom took her time packing. She's a great dawdler, always the last one out of the house whenever we were going somewhere while the rest of us waited in the car. Of course, she had to dress four children before she dressed herself, but that probably had nothing to do with it.

At Fitzer's, I was curious about the black and white puddings included in the Irish breakfast, so I ordered them, even after the waiter said they were made with either light or dark pork meat and spices. And there they were, small bready nuggets, shining with fat. I took a taste and waited for lightning to strike me dead. Nothing. Which was just as well, since one bite had been plenty. And definitely not worth dying for.

Finally, we left. At the front desk, I noticed that our breakfast had not been added to the bill. The clerk applauded my honesty. I applauded my honesty, having achieved at last one small heroism worthy of Mary Robinson, president of Ireland.

We took a cab back to my apartment, where Phoebe came right over demanding she get breakfast too. I scrambled some eggs and made her toast and the three of us sat at the table and talked. And after a while the front door opened and the kids spilled in, flinging off their jackets, while Frank hugged me and started telling me all the things he wanted to do that afternoon. And Mom said she really should go, and Phoebe did too. And everyone kissed good-bye and the kids went off to play in their room and Frank said, "Let's go pick up some stuff for dinner." And we did, walking in the crisp air as he talked, so glad to see me.

As I was him. I linked my arm in his, feeling him warm inside his jacket. And at the corner, while we waited for the light to change, I saw a sign for fresh turkeys and a display of cranberry sauce. And I resolved that this year at Thanksgiving, I would make it a point to save some room and eat Mom's brisket myself.

chapter four

Followed by the Moon

One of the places I know Mom would want to escape to is the moon. Literally. It was always a dream of hers to go there. As a teenager, she even added her name to a list at the American Museum of Natural History, hoping to be among the new generation of astronaut travelers.

She loved all sorts of science. When she was a junior in high school, she lectured on radioactive iodine at an exhibition on behalf of the Atomic Energy Commission to educate the public. I found this impressive, if not downright shocking. When I was a junior in high school, I was cutting first period and eating breakfast at the International House of Pancakes. The closest I had come to delineating a career goal was in the third grade, when we had to draw pictures of ourselves grown up, in our dream jobs. I drew myself behind the counter at Feitlin's, the delicatessen we went to every Sunday night. It seemed a destination of infinite possibility, even though I had the same thing each time, a hot dog and french fries. Mom had center-cut tongue on rye with coleslaw and Russian dressing and a cup of tea with lemon.

After my deli clerk aspiration faded, I wanted to be a ballerina and an actress. Mom, of course, had wanted to be a scientist. The only difficulty she faced was that no one else wanted her to. When she enrolled at the University of Wisconsin in 1949 and declared herself a biochemistry major she was laughed out of the department chairman's office. It was an inappropriate field for women, he scolded. Well, she said, she was willing to be inappropriate. (Boy, have times changed.) Which was when he came right out and said he "would prefer not to have any women in his program" at all.

I always hated this story, and every time I heard it I felt depressed, then livid all over again. And I would launch my usual barrage of irritating questions, along the lines of how-could-he-get-away-with-this. "He didn't have to give a reason," Mom would say. "At that time there was no such thing as sex discrimination. I was very intimidated and decided to look around and see what other field would accept women. Psychology did."

The idea that Mom would be intimidated by an academic bureaucrat saddened me as much as her biochemical road not taken. I know things were different then, for women and for everyone. But intimidation was not a behavior that was ever nurtured in my life. Both my parents advocated a stance of never-give-up, perhaps hoping that our results would be happier. And I think they were right. It seems so difficult for people to say no. It's every two-year-old's favorite word, but when he or she tries it and meets with such opposition from the giants in residence, each learns not to use it again.

So psychology it was for Mom, even though she flirted with nursing (Grandma wouldn't hear of it, though, too many germs). And having chosen her field, she immersed herself in it. While other kids' mothers limited themselves to beaming approval over a pretty picture or a good report card, Mom operated on a higher plane.

Like the time we were driving on the highway and I looked out of the window, up at the night sky. "Look, Mommy," I said, "the moon is following us!" Did she smile sweetly and say, "Yes, darling, it certainly is"? Not exactly. She turned in her seat, her expression thoughtful. "Very good," she murmured, almost to herself. "You are exactly on course at Piaget's preoperational level of development." I didn't know what she meant, of course, but I knew that if Piaget approved it must be good. That was the kind of watch she wore when she got dressed up.

As Mom and I got older, her interest in all things scientific continued to grow while mine held firm at nonexistent, despite her prodding. Which mainly consisted of trips to the American Museum of Natural History, where we could see dinosaurs, dinosaurs and more dinosaurs. Then there were lessons in photosynthesis, which was popular in the spring and summer while the garden was in bloom. And seemingly endless black-and-white footage of Cape Canaveral, accompanied by her all but unintelligible explanations of gravity.

I absolutely couldn't stand it. Even in school, when it was time for science I was reading *Jo's Boys* under the desk. By the time I got to high school, I had taken to hysteria.

In tenth grade my biology teacher was Mr. Ricci, a genuinely nice man who no doubt went home at night questioning his life's work whenever he had me in class. He would ask about whatever—frog skeletons—and I would look at him and laugh. I wasn't trying to be rude, I truly had no idea what he was talking about. The frog could be on the slab right in front of me and I still wouldn't know. And the weight of all the rest of the eyes in the class was just too much. So I laughed. And kept going until the tears streamed and I gasped for air and the other kids joined in and even Mr. Ricci's mouth began to twitch, and he started in too.

Twice, however, he did not. The first time was when we all had painstakingly attached some kind of fly to little squares of tissue paper and set them out on the counter. Then came a fire drill, which I'm quite convinced was to blame for my shattered concentration. Because when we came back, I was so fixated on water, the idea of water, that I turned on the faucet in the nearby sink without noticing that a very dry, very hard sponge lay at the bottom. So when the water hit, it bounced off and flew over the counter, whipping up a little storm of fly-infested tissue-paper squares, ultimately soaking them past the point of usefulness.

Then, I'm sorry to say, I broke a microscope. To this day I can't tell you how, but I grabbed it wrong (maybe I thought I had to shake its hand like a tennis racket, another pastime that passed me by) and Mr. Ricci sent me straight to detention. There was a note home and some solemn words on parent-teacher night, though he very nicely didn't charge me for the instrument's repair. (Dad's Scarsdale tax dollars at work.) When I made it to eleventh grade, no one was more relieved than Mr. Ricci. He knew he would never find me in his AP class.

In college I suffered through one semester of required science (chemistry) and gratefully forgot it all the moment it ended. Then, in my junior year, Margaret Mead, the anthropologist, was chosen to be the commencement speaker. I was on the phone to Mom in a flash, who had idolized her all her life: a woman who had overcome her estrogen and become a scientist anyway.

She drove up to the campus to see her. But as the procession of graduates started and she saw Margaret Mead leading the line, she said, "Oh," as if someone had punched her in the stomach, pushing out a pocket of air. And started to cry.

"Mom, what's wrong?" I had asked. "This is what you were waiting for."

"She's so old," she said sadly, as Dr. Mead walked by, shrunken with age and carrying a walking stick as tall as she was. Once she started speaking, however, her voice and delivery strong, Mom calmed down. And was sufficiently inspired to buy a walking stick of her own, which she located in the wilds of Greenwich, Connecticut. It was polished and very beautiful and conveniently came apart in two pieces, so that if she needed to pack it she could, rather than walk through airports and train stations looking like Moses in a mink.

Not that she needed a walking stick, of course. It was simply an affectation. On the other hand, maybe she did need it. The one thing about my mother you would never know is that she had polio as a child. She has walked without a limp for as long as I've known her, though she sometimes buys two pairs of shoes in two different sizes in order to get one usable pair. And when she comes to the city for theater and dinner, it goes without saying that the distance between the two places should be short enough so she can walk there without difficulty. She says she always has to pay attention to walking so she doesn't trip, but if she really does, I've never caught her at it.

She has fallen, on occasion, but almost never with witnesses, and she would admit it afterward only to explain a bruise. I remember the very first time I realized there was something different about Mom. I was five or six years old and playing with some kids down the block. They started making raucous fun of a reclusive teenager in a wheel-chair, who lived a few houses away and was making a rare appearance that morning in his driveway. When I told Mom about it, fully expecting that she would laugh too, I had the surprise of my life. She turned on me with a venom I had never seen. Then she continued getting ready for work. Standing in front of the mirror she combed her hair, teased and sprayed it, sobbing the entire time.

It was in a municipal pool that she had contracted the disease. When she was three years old, Grandma had taken her swimming one day and before she even knew what happened, Mom was hospitalized and quarantined, not allowed to see her parents for months. And as she got older, she needed a series of operations that finally ended when she was sixteen.

It doesn't take a genius to recognize Grandma's guilt. Her overriding reach for the aesthetic ideal in life was no accident. Yes, she had the great eye, the one Phoebe inherited. But everything in her house was mercilessly controlled, from the precision of her crossword puzzles to the immaculately wrapped containers of garbage she placed in the dumbwaiter. And in the face of all this order, which soon included two hugely handsome, healthy sons, was a daughter who was not only physically imperfect, but who wanted to study biochemistry instead of marrying Izzy Twersky, the rabbi's son. Anatevka, you ask? No, Eastburn Avenue in the Bronx.

Mom reacted as any good (eldest!) daughter would. She wanted to protect her mother, ease her conscience, assure her that she still loved her. And was desperate for Grandma to return the favor. Which she did, sort of. With just enough reservation to always keep Mom guessing about who Grandma was angrier at that she had gotten sick. I think nothing ever made Mom feel more alone than that ambivalence. And ever since I could understand it, I've been trying to fix it.

Not that Mom particularly needed my help. She became the master of overcompensation all by herself. Normal wasn't good enough. Only extraordinary would do. Of course she lectured for the Atomic Energy Commission, and the moon was her ideal travel destination. She never said no, never got tired. Four children, a doctorate, teaching, counseling, reading to the blind. She was the one on her knees with a toothbrush going over the tiles in the bathroom. She cooked all the meals, making blintzes from scratch and potato pancakes for the holidays. In her garden, she grew roses and lilacs and zucchini. If she ever lay down in the middle of the day for a nap, the kids posted a frantic SOS. It was like a horse lying down. She drove herself so harshly in the quest for perfection. And conformity. To seem like everyone else, be accepted by everyone else, in spite of her odd quirks of spirit. Being too different worried her. She'd already been too different. And she knew it wasn't all it was cracked up to be.

Little things throw her. When Phoebe got a tattoo (a lily, on her right upper back), Mom burst into tears.

"What is your problem?" Phoebe genuinely wanted to know.

"You were perfect," Mom cried. "When I gave birth to you you were healthy and whole and unblemished. And now you go and do this."

Phoebe, of course, had assumed that a tattoo would be nothing more than a piece of permanent jewelry. Or a picture of it. But to Mom, well. It truly meant something else.

I hadn't actually seen the walking stick in years, now that I thought about it. But it was Margaret Mead, in fact, who rekindled Mom's interest in taking yet another field trip to the Museum of Natural History, to see its recently opened Margaret Mead Hall of Pacific Peoples. Though Emmett had become Mom's willing companion on her scientific explorations, he was off at Stanford now, so naturally I volunteered for the job. I lived on the Upper West Side, and would pass the museum and marvel at its haunting grandeur without even a trace of dinosaur desperation. It looked like a magnificent castle to me, and I started to wonder, now that I was an adult, if perhaps this science thing was something I could grow into. I mean, not that I have to become my mother, but I'd certainly had enough of the Egyptians at the Met, God knows. Also, there was a *Star Trek* exhibit going on at the Museum of Natural History now, and next to Margaret Mead, Mom loves *Star Trek* best.

When the day arrived and we stood, side by side, surveying a long loop of bones that was a python skeleton and I said, "Disgusting," I was not surprised to hear her say, "Beautiful. You have to be in awe of all these species."

I felt the old claustrophobia coming on. The size and scope of the building notwithstanding, it was getting very close in there. I flashed onto two childhood visits in particular. The first was a third-grade field trip, during which most of my classmates ate their lunches on the bus. A shining example of discipline, I waited. As a result, all I could think of during that interminable morning was my tuna-fish sandwich. Indian longhouse? Tuna-fish sandwich. Hayden Planetarium? Tuna-fish sandwich. When I finally got to eat it, warm and soggy on Wonder bread, I thought I had never tasted anything so sublime in my entire eight years on earth. Since then, it has remained the Proustian standard by which all other food pales. Something about the bag it was in, or the orange drink that went with it, or maybe just the view of Jonathan Mink, the cutest boy in the class, as I ate it.

The second memory, yet another attempt at piquing my scientific interests, came one Sunday afternoon when Mom felt industrious enough to take Greg and me on a field trip herself. There were endless showcases of birds and fish. Endless vistas of towering bones. Endless explanations from Mom, delivered with impressive vigor. And all I could think about was the Automat, where we were going afterward. A place, she said, where you could put a quarter in the wall, open a door and take out the food you wanted. (We took franks and beans. Feitlin's reputation was safe.)

Okay, this was now, and I would stop thinking about food. I was an adult—chronologically, at least—which was why I could no longer plan what outfit Barbie would wear once I got home, so I might as well concentrate. I could, at long last, discover the dormant science gene within and change my life.

Mom was oblivious to my inner battle, already circling the barosaurus. I followed her, ogling too, feeling proud. I was indeed grown up and open to new interests, and the majesty, the stark grace of these bones moved me, deeply, primally, perhaps changing the way I would look at the world forever.

A group of school children ran into the hall.

"Is it time to eat?" one boy asked the teacher. "I'm starving."
"No," she replied. "We don't eat until twelve-fifty."
That was more than an hour away. He was crestfallen.
"I'm hungry too," the teacher admitted.
Well, come to think of it, so was I.
No! I was not going to do this again. I was not going to think about the tuna-fish sandwich Mom had brought today, and I was not going to get sidetracked by the memory of that third-grade tuna-fish sandwich. Or was I? I looked at my watch. We'd been here all of ten minutes. That was enough majesty for anyone. I had obviously been wrong about this. Maybe we could leave and go to Bloomingdale's. We certainly couldn't go to the Automat, which had gone out of business years ago.

Mom reluctantly tore herself away from a detailed explanation of barosaurus vertebrae and shook her head disapprovingly at my lack of commitment to the task at hand. The task, she reminded me, I had so enthusiastically agreed to.

"Poorly, poorly arranged," she lamented, studying a map of the museum. More children went by.

"We going to go eat?" one asked a teacher.

I looked at Mom hopefully. Nothing doing. She wanted to see the Margaret Mead Hall of Pacific Peoples, *and* the *Star Trek* exhibit, *and* the *Star Trek* show in the Planetarium *and* the Hall of Minerals and Gems. For starters. We headed down a dark hallway.

There were dead animals everywhere. Goatsuckers. Titmice. Regular mice. MAMMALS OF NEW YORK STATE read a sign near an all-star line-up of rodents, all of whom looked as if they lived in my old apartment on Bleecker Street. Then there were dead stuffed birds. Hundreds of them. One baby ate out of its mother's mouth, which all but enveloped its head. Who's eating whom here? I asked. Mom was unamused.

After thirty minutes of wrong turns we found Margaret Mead and the Pacific Peoples. Among the tribal artifacts, the display cases contained a pad entitled "Reporter's Notebook, Samoa 1925–26." Finally, something I could appreciate. Maybe staying wouldn't be so bad. Mom was thrilled, and lunchtime approached.

We found a gift shop. "Food, food, food," chanted three boys who ran in past us. They dug into a large basket and pulled out a foil package of freeze-dried ice cream.

"Cool!" they shouted, before running out again to try it. Mom couldn't resist buying one herself. It went into my bag, next to the sandwich.

Time for the *Star Trek* show. But how to find it? We ventured down more shadowy hallways. "I hear an elevator bell," Mom said, triumphant. "You have to use all your senses in this place to get around."

Once the program began I was convinced we were in the wrong place. I assumed I would see Captain Kirk on the Planetarium ceiling, but this confusing display of constellations looked exactly like the one I saw the last time I was here. The little boy next to me fell asleep. Even Mom was restless.

The exhibit was better. Mr. Spock's makeup-encrusted latex ear tips, which had been worn by the actor Leonard Nimoy, were in a glass box. And there was a video about the show. In it, one of the producers announced that *Star Trek* was not an action adventure series, but a morality play about the Ten Commandments. Really? All those years of Hebrew School and all I needed to do was watch *Star Trek*? Damn.

Mom insisted on sitting in Captain Kirk's chair. And not just sitting in it, but planting her feet and resting each arm on the control panels, the way he did. It was one of those moments where, if you were thirteen, you would die, even if there were only strangers in the room. But as a mature adult I was not at all embarrassed. Possibly because I stayed at the opposite end of the room with my back turned.

It was almost 3:00 P.M. and the Morgan Memorial Hall of Gems and Minerals was still ahead. Walking to Pittsburgh would have been easier. But once we were stationed in front of the sixty-carat Armstrong diamond necklace, Mom couldn't have been happier. I wanted my sandwich.

Which I had, *finally*. It certainly was delicious, but not even close to the original. First of all, seven-grain health bread did not get soggy the way Wonder bread, with its great Play-Doh consistency, did. And nowadays there were grown-up ingredients in the tuna-fish, like dill and white pepper. Too fancy. And this sandwich had lettuce. It didn't use to have lettuce. It also used to be cut into four pieces, so it seemed to last longer.

The freeze-dried ice cream was unspeakable. Something along the lines of Necco wafers, with a rancid aftertaste. Remember those vile things? Candy from grown-ups who hated children.

It was 4:00 P.M. by the time we left. Mom was elated. A day among the species was a day well spent. We walked into the November wind and my ankle started to hurt. She noticed the change in my walk immediately. Why? she asked me, even though she knew.

About a year after I got married, I was on the treadmill one day and my left ankle felt bothered. I thought I'd sprained or strained it and called the doctor, who examined me and diagnosed a chronic ligament problem from overuse. He told me to stop working out for six weeks and let it rest. The first problem with this advice was that the doctor was my friend Philip's brother, Stephen, whom I had grown up with. He had been in Greg's grade, and I had a hard time taking him seriously. Their father, James Nicholas, was a world-famous orthopedist who had treated President Kennedy's back and Joe Namath's knees. If he had told me to stop, I would have listened. But Stephen? I didn't remember him in diapers, but close.

The second problem with this advice was that he might as well have told me to stop breathing. Not that I love exercise. I view it only as the necessary evil it is to keep weight off, with the intermittent benefit of an endorphin rush that lets me ride the subways without committing homicide. Compulsions are my life. I couldn't just stop. And God knows, the memory of those ninth-grade hips is a powerful one.

So I rested for a day and went right back on the treadmill and the StairMaster and the rowing machine. When my ankle hurt, I skipped a day, thinking that would be enough rest, then went back. Weeks passed. It got worse. I stopped using the machines and walked in the pool instead. That was a real treat, trying to avoid the type A swimmers who even found their way to the "slow" lane. Stephen had also told me to stop wearing shoes with three-inch heels, and finally I did. During the day. But at night, there they were.

It kept getting worse. I tried ice. I tried heat. I kept my foot elevated. The ankle grew thicker. I tried mind over body. "It's only an ankle, what's the big deal? It's not broken. I'm resting it enough. I sit at a desk all day, after all." I took extra Advil. I drank extra wine with dinner. Then I started waking up in the middle of the night. The pressure of the sheet and blankets was bothering it. I slept with an Ace bandage. It still hurt.

Three months later, Stephen had had enough. "I'm going to have to immobilize you since you won't immobilize yourself," he said, and had me fitted for a walking cast, which meant I could take it off to shower but still had to sleep with it. By that point, I couldn't argue. I needed a cab just to take me the three blocks to the video store.

"You see, you overdo everything!" Mom yelled, when I told her.

"I? *I* overdo everything?" I yelled back. "Where could I possibly have learned that from?"

It just galled me to ever say no to anything, to ever cry uncle. (And where could I possibly have learned *that* from?) The worst part about it was that my body was going ahead and doing whatever it wanted to without me. I was scared.

The three months I spent in the cast seemed to last forever. My ankle grew smaller and so did my leg. Atrophy is the word for it, since none of the muscles was being used. Then came weeks of physical therapy. I strengthened my leg, but the ankle did not improve. Finally, Stephen had to inject the ligament itself.

"I guess I should have listened to you at the beginning," I said halfheartedly; Phoebe had come along to hold my hand and I buried my head in her lap. To his eternal credit, Stephen was gracious about it. I was the asshole who had never gotten past the hierarchy of high school.

He had to give me another shot a few months later, which was followed by six more months of weakness, pain, inactivity and utter defeat. After it had been going on for over a year, I woke up one morning and started to cry and couldn't stop until the evening. I felt thoroughly broken. And it was then I realized that it was my left foot that wasn't working properly. And that it's Mom's left foot that doesn't work properly either. Then I was doubly scared. Was I so anxious about getting married and leaving her that I had made myself her Siamese twin, joined for eternity at the foot? Because that way we would still be together? If it happened to both of us, she couldn't be alone. And neither could I.

I guess it had been mind over body the whole time. I just hadn't known it.

So, now, as we walked, I reassured her that I had just started a brand-new round of physical therapy with a terrific guy who treated dancers and was very big on the mind-body connection. He didn't think there was anything wrong with my ankle that couldn't be fixed with a little strengthening. Physical and mental.

I told her that spending the whole day on those marble museum floors had just aggravated it. No big deal. Then she admitted that she had felt it (only a little!) too.

We found a phone because it was time, naturally, to call Phoebe, who was at work, and arranged to meet for tea at the Fitzpatrick, which was near her gallery. And there we were, back again, while Mom and Phoebe ate sandwiches and I watched, still full from my late lunch. I had to leave soon, anyway, to meet Frank. Mom was telling her everything about the museum, taking real pleasure in all the descriptions.

Maybe it was okay, I thought, that she hadn't become a biochemist after all, because she has science as a hobby and if it was her job she wouldn't enjoy it the same way. But she probably wouldn't mind that, and I knew it. And then I thought that I was glad I was so bad in science after all, because I could keep her company. Neither one of us could be a scientist together.

I kissed them both good-bye and left them there, talking. Once I was out on the street, I started walking very fast, making all the lights. And I thought about that, about walking so easily, so early in this new round of physical therapy and I wondered if I would be okay this time. And I thought about Mom and how that museum today had been such a touchstone in her life for so many years. How each time she went there she must secretly wonder what had happened to that list of volunteers who wanted to fly to the moon. And where they had gone instead.

I looked up. Yes, there was the moon, not quite full and bright as a streetlamp. Though traveling there would be the last thing I'd want, no matter how much Mom loves it.

I looked at it some more. Hey! It was still following me!

Uh-oh. Mom would not be pleased to hear that. I crossed the street and my ankle twinged. Or maybe she would.

chapter five

A World Full of Megs

ow to describe Scarsdale? Picture this: a Cadillac that takes up three parking spaces instead of one; a kid who takes an hour to sign someone's yearbook and then asks for it back so he can copy the message, so blinded by its brilliance was he in retrospect; a fifteen-year-old boy having sex with his family's live-in maid.

Entitlement was the motto of this affluent town. The women would slice your face to get a hot bestseller from the library ahead of you. The men were barely glimpsed, rising predawn and coming home past dark, and the good Lord only knows what they were actually doing in the big city besides their jobs.

In Scarsdale schools, the goal was popularity, which meant you had dates arranged a week in advance with the "in" group of girls, who would only be seen with the "in" group of guys. A car was standard issue for every kid (Porsches were hot), as were allowances that could buy the best pot on the market, with plenty left over for cocktails.

What was really special, though, were the contacts, which meant you had to know the lineage of your playmates up front or your time was in danger of being wasted. On my first day in seventh grade at the Quaker Ridge School, I was invited to sit with a group of girls in gym class. They went around in a circle, each one telling me her name and what her father did for a living (none of their mothers seemed to do anything worth mentioning). What did my father do? they demanded. Well, I knew the correct answer was to say that he worked on Wall Street, even though his office was on Madison Avenue, a discrepancy that bothered me no end, but there it was. Thankfully, as these things went, Wall Street seemed perfectly acceptable, though certainly not as dazzling as being Vicki Gifford's father. (Pre–Kathie Lee. Pre-pre–Kathie Lee.)

So I made the first cut. And Susan Edbril invited me to her birthday party. (Victory!) After a few not-so-subtle stares, I left my kneesocks at home and had all my skirts shortened to fingertip length, like everybody else. Because that was key. Being different wouldn't just be humiliating. It would mean utter failure.

Of course, there were local celebrities. The Marx family, the owners of the toy company, had a huge estate that made for the best trick-or-treating on Halloweeen because instead of candy they gave out toys. Roberta Peters, the opera singer, could be spotted on occasion, shopping at Gristedes. And the pièce de résistance was Dr. Herman Tarnower, the famed Scarsdale Diet doctor, who practiced at the Scarsdale Medical Center.

Later, as history unfolded, you could hear the villagers (Scarsdale is a village—isn't that cute?) boast about their inside information on Lynne Tryforos, the nurse, the other woman, over whom Jean Harris had grown so distraught. They had seen the body language between her and the doctor, they claimed. They could have predicted what would happen. Very full of himself, he was. I had never seen him in person, actually. He was a doctor for grown-ups and I still had a pediatrician. But in his pictures he looked to me like he had eaten one too many of his prescribed Monday lunches—tuna with vinegar and lemon juice.

I was squarely on Jean Harris's side. As was Mom, though she had reservations, of course. She wasn't condoning murder, she wanted me to know. Heaven forbid I should choose Jean Harris as a role model. The grammar and syntax might have been perfect but the aim was lousy. And she had failed as an educator. She had the chance to instruct a generation of girls on how to stage a suicide scene with the elegance of Madame Butterfly, only to bungle it with the ham-fisted heat of Danielle Steel.

But it was the fact that she was the headmistress of the exclusive Madeira School, Mom pointed out, that really worked against her. She was smarter than her jurors, and they not only knew it, but resented it. She had lost before she started.

I agreed. But what bothered me was not the jury but Jean Harris's taste in men. This was all his fault.

Since then, there hasn't been another big scandal in Scarsdale. Leona Helmsley came closest, living in Greenwich, Connecticut. But by that time, a decade later, when the Queen of the Helmsley Palace was convicted for tax evasion and mail fraud, Mom seemed less judgmental. The fact that she hadn't murdered anyone seemed to help. And she did pay more than $8 million in fines and restitution. People just didn't like her, Mom said, because she was tough and a woman. And that wasn't fair.

Sure it wasn't. But at least Leona's guy didn't cheat on her. They cheated other people, together.

Philip's mom actually knew Leona Helmsley and used to go to her "I'm Just Wild About Harry" birthday parties every year. She would tell me how much Mrs. Helmsley really loved him, what a generous and caring wife she was. She told of tears Mrs. Helmsley shed over her son's early death and portrayed her as a genuinely grieving mother.

I had seen Mrs. Helmsley myself once in a theater lobby. It was an opening night, or at least I assume it was, since my memory of her was regal indeed, in an elaborate evening gown with a fur-trimmed matching coat. Her face looked as smooth as the marble in her bathrooms.

I was tempted to walk up to her and ask where she had gotten her gown. I had my suspicions, since I had once tried to get Leona Helmsley a free Chanel suit.

It was the mid 1980s, at the beginning of my illustrious career in publishing, as the secretary to the editor in chief at *Elle* magazine. My boss had met Mrs. Helmsley at a party, and the prospect of a deep and meaningful friendship loomed large for them both; visions of (free) hotel suites danced through the editor's head, as visions of (free) outfits bloomed for the queen. So, guess whose job it was to call and try to convince the PR department to let loose the suit?

It took the House of Chanel no time at all to decide its fortunes were solid enough without the modeling finesse of Mrs. Helmsley, queen or no queen. So much for that friendship.

I actually never thought of using other women to get things in the name of friendship. As I grew up, there seemed to be such a code of honor about being a friend, something that was wrapped up in trust and secrets and a sense of home that someone else could snuggle into whenever they told you their news. (At least it was after that initial Scarsdale evaluation, once it was determined you were worth the time and effort.) And then, girls were so loyal. They would always be there for each other if a boy ever did a bad thing, which was always. They would band together. I wonder why, then, so many of my best friends have been men.

I think a lot of the time I just didn't want someone else's secrets snuggling into me. I didn't have room for myself. I wanted to get out of the Women and Children First group and see what else was out there. When I was little and my father would take Greg and me horseback riding, my favorite part was the gallop, when I was told a hundred times to be extra careful. It was just me and the horse and I liked it that way, leaving the others in the dust. Not that I was ever much of an athlete. I'd spend most of my time reading. "Girls who read are dangerous!" my father would chide, fancying himself the soul of wit.

Well, he was right, I discovered. Because girls who read find out that boys get the better deal, whether they read or not. Sure, when I was in high school I always liked going shopping with the girls and driving by the houses of all the boys we had crushes on, squealing at the possibility (oh my God!) that they would be outside at just that moment and see us. But I can't ever say that I looked at my friends who were girls and wanted to be just like them, since most wanted husbands, babies and tennis lessons. Yes, they would have a career before the kids, and maybe even after. But, like a spring coat, it was something they would put away, to wait its turn. (Haven't you heard, girls? We don't get spring anymore.)

Much as I wanted to be like everybody else, I also wanted to be like no one else. Special. Unique. Apart. I wanted the love and acceptance of conformity with all the thrill-seeking uplift of the renegade. I would not grow up and get married and have children like everybody else. I would grow up and do something so extraordinary that my biography would be in the children's section of the library, my home away from home.

I remember, one day, reading the biography of Lucretia Mott, an early American feminist. I was wearing a red dress with a white collar that had a huge rooster printed on it (Mom's potholder motif at work). The dress had a little bow on each side, for decoration. I was reading the book and thinking how wonderful it would be to grow up to be spirited, independent, a leader of women. (That's what my name, Alexandra, meant, Mom would tell me. Though any time she called me that, it was usually because I had accomplished something bad enough to disgrace women everywhere.)

I noticed then that one of the bows had gotten stuck in between the metal arm and plastic cushion of the rec-room couch. Not a problem for a future feminist of America. I yanked it free, with great determination, hearing crowds cheer my decisiveness.

I examined my triumphant expression in the reflection of the window at great length before looking down. I had ripped the bow off the dress. It seemed to have been anchored to a reinforced seam that was now pulled inside out and alarmingly white. With all the spirit and courage of a future feminist leader I went to my mother and told her that a boy in school pulled the bow off my dress and it wasn't my fault. (She believed me.) Plenty of time to be spirited later on.

Of course nowadays it's fashionable to hear sayings like "How do you expect a good girl to grow up to be a great woman?" Well, of course, you sort of can't. But you can't tell girls that. They'd never behave. And since boys never do anyway, no one would be accountable.

The two women I always revered as role models were Eleanor Roosevelt and Annie Sullivan. Mom had Eleanor Roosevelt too. Being her husband's legs went a long way with her. For me, I think it was the image of Eleanor as a little girl, walking up and down her grandmother's driveway with a broom hooked through her arms to improve her posture. (I read her biography in the children's section of the library over and over.) Her mother thought she was so terribly plain, the book said. As I grew up, I learned that meant ugly. And I thought how awful it would be to have a mother who not only thought her own child was ugly, but told her so.

Then there was Annie Sullivan. Talk about conquering the impossible! I thought she, mostly in the person of Anne Bancroft, was the greatest. Not to mention Jo, from *Little Women*, though, granted she was a fictional character. Spirited, independent, always writing. Not great-looking, but great-thinking, cutting off her hair to get money for Marmee. Besides, what were the other choices? Meg was obedient, Amy was vain, Beth was dead. It had to be Jo. I too, I pledged, would grow up to keep my family together, write books, shear my hair and the world be damned.

But what happens when you grow up trying to be like Jo in a world full of Megs? No one likes you for it. They suspect you. Why are you working all the time? Why aren't you dating more? Are you lucky? Or cursed? Girls like Meg grow up to have husbands, children and lunch dates at the club. Girls like Jo grow up to have books and no hair.

Unfortunately, Mom was never much help on this issue. A Jo at heart, she was raised in a generation and a family that insisted on Meg. So she was both, depending on the day. Jo in theory, Meg in practice. As I said, not much help.

But, oddly enough, my father was. Because for all his perfectionism, his win-or-die-this-minute philosophy, he extended it as equally to Mom and Phoebe and me as he did to himself and the boys. He encouraged Mom to get her PhD. He encouraged her to have a career. He made it seem that I could do anything any boy could do. Never mind our having to set the table at home. Out there, anything was possible. He had great disdain for women who went to college and didn't do something wonderful with their education. The world he presented to me was one I could explore, one in which I could find great things, do great things.

And I liked that idea, in spite of the fact that he too sent a double message. Because, just by the way, he also wanted grandchildren and a place to eat dinner on Sunday nights. He somehow thought I could be Amelia Earhart and Molly Goldberg at the same time. Like Mom— great in theory, a little fuzzy on the details. So I accepted the part of the message that I liked—the world part, not the home-and-babies part. I didn't want to miss anything. The day after I was born my parents brought me home from the hospital and Mom said I was sticking my head out of the carriage trying to hear their conversation. See? It was destiny.

But it was surprisingly hard to find men of my own generation who agreed with my father. I dated a guy once who worked on Wall Street, doing God knows what. Actually, he was a friend of the Alexander's heir, and I liked him all right. I was still working at *Elle,* having become its entertainment editor, so I had to see a lot of movies. Not too terrible a job description, I thought.

For our first date, I asked the Wall Street guy to come to a screening of *Crossing Delancey.* On our second date, I asked him to a screening of *Big.* On our third date, there were no screenings, so we went to get sushi. And no sooner had we settled down to dinner, than he turned to me with a huge sigh of relief, unmistakably tinged with pent-up annoyance, and said, "Well, at least we don't have to do your work tonight."

And I thought, that's just swell. It was such a hardship, to see movies like these? It wasn't exactly as if I was making him sit through nine hours of *Shoah.* And I knew, as I watched him chew his eel, that this guy was absolutely off the program. My "three dates and you're out or I sleep with you" policy determined that this was one Wall Street executive who was going to sleep alone that night. Jerk.

Mom was sympathetic to my plight. If anything, she might have wanted Dad to be a little less energetic in pushing her career pursuits. She pushed herself hard enough. But the autonomy he encouraged was crucial for her. So many other careerless women in Scarsdale were thoroughly controlled by their husbands. The summer before I went to college, I worked as a cashier at one of the local supermarkets and was actually given checks for thirty-nine cents from women whose husbands demanded an accounting of every single expenditure, even if they had forgotten the cucumber for that night's salad.

Phoebe would never put up with that kind of life, even though her man search did not necessarily include someone supportive of her career. She wasn't sure she really wanted one. And though she was certainly more charitable about the Scarsdale women who didn't work than either Mom or me, she had no interest in being controlled by anyone.

As for her role models, Phoebe had no use for Eleanor Roosevelt. She chose the Bionic Woman, Mom and me.

I never watched *The Bionic Woman*, but I got the drift. And yes, of course Mom was a role model for me too. All my friends in high school loved Mom. She treated them like adults, advised them when they fought with their parents and when their parents fought with each other. She supervised trips to Planned Parenthood for birth control information when girls were afraid to ask their mothers' gynecologists. She encouraged everyone to go to graduate school. She took them seriously.

But *me* as a role model? That I had a harder time with. To me, a role model is someone who always knows what's right. Infallible. Well, almost. Even Marmee couldn't make Beth live.

The old-fashioned version of a role model was setting a good example. I remember a number of conversations with my ninth-grade English teacher, Miss Dodge, on this very topic. I told her that my parents were sooooo unfair because they wouldn't let me drive cross-country with two boys from camp. Miss Dodge did not approve of this idea either. She told me to imagine that every action of mine was like dropping a stone in a pond, sending ever-widening circles to the edges. "Every action has its consequence" was her point, seeming to imply that I would ruin the lives of any other fifteen-year-old girl who saw me traveling with two aspiring hippies because they would also feel they could turn their backs on Socrates and Emily Dickinson and drive toward Haight-Ashbury without having any place to stop and shower.

I didn't go. Plenty of time to be spirited later on. But when is later? And how fine a line is there between spirited and dangerous? Spirited and rude? Spirited and wrong-headed?

Granted, between Jean Harris and Leona Helmsley, and Eleanor Roosevelt and Annie Sullivan, there's room for almost every woman who's ever lived, me included. But learning how to integrate the two sides of the double message was hard. Some days I wanted nothing more than to stay home and make soup. Other days the idea of home stifled and I wanted to get on a plane and go. Which is what I ended up doing. A story in Indiana? Texas? Iowa? Sure. The soup could wait.

Eventually, Leona Helmsley found herself at the Federal prison in Danbury, Connecticut, and I sort of forgot about her. I did hear she was paying other people to make her bed, but what the hell? Some habits die hard.

One day she reappeared, transferred to a halfway house in midtown Manhattan. I read a description of the lobby there that seemed to focus on a forlorn plant in the corner, to show how the mighty had fallen, and I actually thought about going. I even looked up the address of the place. A few weeks passed and I read that she was to finish her sentence at the Park Lane Hotel, her actual residence, where she would have a curfew of 9:00 P.M. Aha! I felt a story coming on.

So, it was only 6:00 P.M. Where was she?

Not here in the lobby, filled with crystal, marble and lots of security. And me, waiting for Mom. We were going to spend the weekend, which, it turned out, was the last one of Mrs. Helmsley's home confinement. Time really flies when you're not the one in jail.

Why was I here? What was I looking for? I didn't really know. Maybe I wanted to see ruin. Or transcendence. Maybe a lesson would be waiting on Mrs. Helmsley's face that couldn't be learned elsewhere.

A live lab in Women's Studies. Men paced with walkie-talkies, eyeing everyone, me included, with suspicion.

The desk clerk was insistent. She wanted my signature on file. "Are you here with your husband?" she demanded.

"Well, no," I faltered. She seemed to smirk. "I'm here with my mother."

"I'll need her signature on file as well," she said crisply. Finger-prints not required. Here was Mom now, with her green suitcase that used to be my green suitcase before I started living in apartments with no closet space.

Our bellhop warmed quickly to the subject of his employer, the tourist attraction. Even though we were headed to the forty-first floor, he pressed the button for forty-six, where Mrs. Helmsley was jailed in her two-story apartment with swimming pool. When the doors opened, a security guard glared from his post in the hallway. The bellhop apologized profusely as the doors slid shut.

Was she actually in there? He nodded. But with a curfew, right? "It's house arrest, miss. Let's call it what it is," he said amiably. "She's getting ready to go away, I think to Colorado or Arizona for a few months. But she's already been up to her old tricks."

Like what?

"Mean! She hollers at everyone to keep them on their toes. I'm on to her though. I stay out of her way."

He left us in a corner room on the forty-first floor, where the view of Central Park was breathtaking. Though it was already dark, there was plenty to see as the city scrolled out before us: Wollman Memorial Rink dotted with skaters, the trees at Tavern on the Green beaded with lights, the George Washington Bridge sitting at the top of the picture.

And the room was quite welcoming, decorated in calming colors, sea-foam green and cream. We had requested smoking, and there were ashtrays and matches in abundance, as you might expect from a former

Chesterfield Girl, which Mrs. Helmsley became back when she was trying to shed Lena Mindy Rosenthal from Brooklyn.

Between the view, the ashtrays and the room's flattering light, Mom was becoming Leona's biggest champion. Her cab driver claimed to have seen Mrs. Helmsley leave the Park Lane on the morning her imprisonment began. Poor woman, he said, she didn't do anything different from a lot of other people. She had just gotten caught. Mom agreed. "She's an old lady," she said now, with a new tone of indignation. "It's enough."

We got back into the elevator.

"Have you seen Leona yet?" I asked the man and woman inside.

"No," she said brightly, adjusting her mink. "But that is something to look forward to."

"Is she out of the can?" the man growled. "That's real nice, to have a convicted felon running a hotel."

He snorted. She wilted. Staying here must have been her idea.

Still no sign of Leona in the lobby on our way out. We met Phoebe for dinner at Orso to repeat our gabfest. Phoebe had no opinion about Leona Helmsley's criminal exploits, pro or con (so to speak), and had absolutely no interest in seeing her. Her only question was, yet again, why she wasn't staying over.

"Because you should learn to read a newspaper," I said. "How can you not even know what went on with this woman?"

"Well, I think she shouldn't have been so mean to people," Phoebe said valiantly. "But I feel sorry for her too. She's being punished for being tough."

In which case all three of us were in danger of immediate incarceration.

On Saturday morning Mom and I ordered breakfast from room service so we wouldn't have to leave our view. The continental breakfast offered a bread basket that included a brioche. Mom has a thing about brioches. She loves them and she can never find one fresh enough or light enough. She scorns loaves and wants only the individual ones with the buttons on top. She gets into these quests every once in a while where she sets her sights on a single peculiar thing and has to find the best. I had a boyfriend like that once too. He was on a quest for the perfect White Russian. The only problem was he drank so many he never remembered where the good ones were.

This brioche was only average, so we vowed that later in the day we would try Ecce Panis, a chic Upper East Side bakery. For now, there was the view. Two horse-drawn carriages made their way slowly past heaps of snow and a frosted gazebo. Mom poured herself tea from a small pot after removing the tiny cork in its spout and we shared the morning papers.

I called Frank. This being Saturday, the kids were over and I knew that he missed me. Mom kept her eyes on the paper, pretending not to listen to my conversation. She almost never called Dad when she came away with me. Overall, I think they don't talk to each other half as much as Frank and I do, but we're probably excessive. We work in the same business, after all, for the same company. When one of us has a story about work, the other immediately knows who the characters are and what the implications mean. But work aside, we do seem to talk constantly, about everything and nothing, I guess, though, when one is on deadline the other knows to lay off. When we're both on deadline, well, nothing's perfect.

The fact that Frank took my career seriously went a long way with Mom. She just couldn't understand why I didn't get on with it all, why I needed to have these endless conversations. (Dare I say, fun?) But Mom assumed that because I was career-oriented like her, my marriage would reflect hers. Separate but equal. She used to look at other couples who spent a lot of time together and shudder, as if she couldn't breathe. It felt abhorrent to her to be so wrapped up with someone every second of the day.

I had always assumed that I felt the same way, keeping huge distances between me and my boyfriends, seeing them in their allotted time, and basically forgetting about them when they weren't scheduled. Until Frank. Then I found that I genuinely liked being with someone all the time. Or rather, I liked being with *him* all the time. I think Mom worried about self-sufficiency. She had learned in her own way not to trust people to do too much, care too much, and so she didn't ask, didn't expect. With my dad that seemed to work fine, since they are both of the generation that would prefer not to acknowledge emotions, much less analyze them.

The Girls Only split was for a reason: Mom had her own territory, her own concerns and activities in life that were not to be shared with a husband, or any male. As her daughters, we were included, but the thing about Mom is that you always suspected she'd just as soon have alone time to do her girl things. Which would make me work even harder to be part of them. Which, of course, is what Phoebe was doing now with me. Or I was doing with Phoebe.

It was noon before I forced myself into the shower. Mom had deemed her gigantic bath towel "a very impressive piece of cloth." I was less impressed by a long black hair on each side of the tub, considering that Mom is blonde.

My thoughts turned to the Prisoner of Central Park South. Maybe she was wandering the halls now, walking laps for exercise. On the other hand, she had a pool up there. She could swim laps in utter privacy. But with the shrimp, or without? I had read once that at the end of each lap she would reach up to a tray of shrimp held by a servant and eat one as a reward. This seemed exotic. In my family you weren't allowed in the pool for a full hour after eating.

I wanted to go up there. I could just pretend I pressed the wrong floor. Or bring a cake with a file inside. (Devil's food?)

And then it came to me. I'd ask for her autograph. She was a celebrity, after all.

I got a pen and a postcard of the Park Lane from the folder on the desk and headed toward the elevator. My heart beat faster. The doors opened. There she'd be and I'd take one look and see it. The reason she went bad, the fatal flaw, the gap between spirit and spite. In the glint of her eyes or the twist of her mouth. Some sign, a lesson, the moral of the story, right there in the penthouse.

But there was only a security guard, a man about sixty, sitting at a table reading a library book. I hemmed and hawed as if it were Madonna in there behind him: I-would-really-be-so-grateful, we're-having-such-a-great-weekend-and-it's-such-a-wonderful-hotel-and-would-she-mind? He stared at me, weary. Apparently, this was not an original idea. And my delivery wasn't exactly Oscar material.

Silence.

"Uhm, does she usually give autographs when people ask?" He shook his head no, sternly. I waited, trying my best to look eager. And innocent.

Finally, he spoke. "If she comes out I can ask her. Write down your room number."

I did.

"What are you reading?" I couldn't help myself.

The blush started around his ears. "Uhm, a detective novel," he admitted. I smiled sweetly. We were even.

I went back to the room and told this all to Mom, who just sighed. Other people's children grew up to be doctors and lawyers.

There was a knock at the door. It was my pal, the security guard. "You can write a note asking for her autograph and put it in an envelope and someone will give it to her secretary and see what she can do. But no promises," he added gruffly. He must have read that line just this morning.

Okay, so I'd write her, but not now. I was starving, Phoebe had arrived and it was almost 2:00 P.M., which meant tea service would begin at the New York Palace, formerly the Helmsley Palace, where we planned to have lunch. In the wake of the family's troubles, the hotel was sold to the sultan of Brunei. At least it went to royalty.

But first we detoured to Ecce Panis, where people were crammed inside the door for the opportunity to pay five dollars for a loaf of bread. I didn't see the individual brioches, which I had called about specifically. "Where are they?" I asked, when it was finally our turn. "Here." The woman pointed to a loaf. Mom shook her head with disgust. She can really get dug in over these things, which is another of the differences between us. I never search for the perfect anything. I know in advance it's not there.

We were the first customers in the Palace's Gold Room. Something was different here. It was too quiet. The harp was gone. The waiter brought menus. Did he ever work for Mrs. Helmsley? No, he was new. "I heard that she was very strict, so the service was excellent," he said. "Now, it's more simple. But still very good," he added quickly.

It was, and so was the food. The chicken-salad sandwiches especially were heaven. Phoebe and I couldn't eat them fast enough. Cucumber and watercress were fresh, the smoked salmon excellent. Servings were unlimited, and you didn't have to chase down a waiter to get more. Before I realized it, I had eaten ten sandwiches. Then scones, with clotted cream.

We talked a lot and laughed. Phoebe was thoroughly enjoying herself. She is able to be in the moment so much more than I can; I'm always planning ahead or worrying behind. Maybe I could actually find it in my small, Grinch-like heart to let her sleep over next time.

I was surprised when Mom's stomach started up as we walked on Fifth Avenue. That hadn't happened lately, at least not that I'd been aware of. Veal. She and Phoebe decided it was the veal she'd had for dinner last night. We went back to the room so she could lie down and Phoebe stayed with her while I wandered through the Park Lane lobby. Its jewelry store advertised an estate sale, with a pretty diamond ring up front, very delicate. A bargain, it would seem, at $1,200. This was something that would make Mom happy. Not for her, for me. I flat out refused a diamond solitaire when I got married, much to her chagrin. "A woman can't have too many diamonds," has always been her motto. "I ride the subways and I want to live," has always been mine. But maybe I could get something like this, for special occasions.

I told Mom about the ring and she wanted to see it for herself, so she trekked downstairs, stomach and all. "Hmmmm," she said quickly, in her diamond-appraising tone, nose wrinkling. "Too small."

Well, that was one less decision for the ages. I could think about dinner instead. We had reserved in the Park Room on the hotel's second floor, where the huge windows looked out onto Central Park and you could see the horse-drawn carriages in close-up. It was one of those increasingly rare places in New York where you feel you've gone back in time.

Frank called. He had taken the kids to Chinatown for lunch and all over the place on errands, and the three of them were good and cranky. Especially him. I took the leap and broke the rule, inviting them for dinner. Mom was suffering with her stomach and Phoebe was suffering from not sleeping over and I was suffering from knowing how much I'd suffer tomorrow when I got home and no one was happy.

So they came. It was an adventure for the kids, who loved the mission of trying to spot an elusive criminal. We trooped into the restaurant, where only two other tables were filled. But, alas, no queen. In one of those books written about her she was described as sitting in the Park Room screaming obscenities at an employee, tuna fish bubbling out of her mouth. Happily, that dish was served only at lunch, but still I had hoped. It was past 9:00 P.M., after all.

We went back to our room to watch the Golden Globe Awards and because a three-course dinner is never enough, Nat and Simon ordered french fries and ice cream from room service. Frank lay on my bed with a headache and I rubbed his forehead. Mom whispered, "Look at his face!" because he looked so genuinely relieved and happy to be there and I started thinking that maybe these Girls Only nights didn't have to be extended to full weekends, that maybe one night at a time would be enough. When they finally left to go home, I felt bad.

The next morning, I took my handwritten plea back up to the forty-sixth floor. The guard was different, a younger man reading the *New York Post*. He barely glanced at the envelope as I explained its contents, tossing it aside like a used napkin.

I headed for the front desk, defeated. As we checked out, Mom noticed a can there for donations to a fund for people with Alzheimer's disease, which affects Harry Helmsley. It was the kind of container you'd expect to see in a deli or a dry cleaner. I thought again about the "I'm Just Wild About Harry" parties. There were bands, Philip's mom said, and balloons.

Mom got a cab. She said she had had a good time, but with so many hours of agony devoted to her stomach, I couldn't imagine how. I kissed her good-bye and walked past the doorman, up the block.

Damn! I felt so frustrated. What had I accomplished? I got Mom down to the city to eat veal and get sick. I left Frank with the kids, had them over anyway, and then when they left I felt even worse. I had forbidden Phoebe, yet again, to be fully included. And the whole point of my *Times* assignment, to find Leona, hadn't even worked. All in all, a slam-bang weekend.

I turned back and squinted up, up toward the penthouse, trying to see if maybe she was there, face pressed to the glass yearning to be free. Lena Mindy Rosenthal, the girl who would be queen. After all those years of deals, of pushing and pulling and scheming and saving and climbing and crawling, there she was, starting over again, at seventy-four, with a husband who might not even recognize her anymore.

I remembered then that I had read somewhere that her best friend was her maid. Who might even be up there now, keeping her company. Listening to the litany of how she had been wronged. Again.

And it occurred to me, standing openmouthed on Central Park South, my neck bent so far back my sunglasses rested on my forehead, that maybe, after all these years, it was the other side of that double message I should have been listening to. That maybe being Jo isn't always the noblest choice. That not every woman needs to be a husband's legs or teach a blind deaf-mute to say *water* to be an exceptional woman. Or fly to Milwaukee, at a moment's notice. Maybe even if you play tennis and have lunch at the club, the fact that you can give someone else a sense of home to snuggle their secrets into is perhaps the best use of a spirit after all. To nurture. Comfort. Reassure. Not just to run. Or jump. High, higher, highest. I hadn't really thought about that part before, in my quest for the next, whatever that may be.

As I got into a cab, I marveled at my tiny view of the world. The truth was, I hadn't needed to come here at all. I already understood far more about Leona Helmsley than I would ever care to admit. It was the maid I should have been looking for. I might actually have learned something.

chapter six

My Pillow

One of the most shocking discoveries of my adult life was that no one but me considered the movie version of *Gypsy* a masterpiece. As a kid I thought there was nothing better. It had everything—mothers, daughters, showbiz, true love, lost love, fame, betrayal, redemption. Even a lamb as a birthday present. Which struck a particular chord with me ever since my sheep escapade of the first grade, which Mom will never let me forget.

My teacher, Mrs. Israel, asked everyone in class about their pets. Well, my father was allergic to dogs and cats, so the closest thing we had was a parakeet named Specksey, after the dog Mom grew up with. To my mind the bird wasn't much of a pet. The only time he fulfilled the role was when his cage was being cleaned and he would escape, flying to the top of the curtain rods, making us spend hours trying to coax him back inside. He apparently tired of this routine as quickly as I did, dropping down dead in his cage one morning. Mom wrapped him in a paper towel and we buried him in the backyard.

This wasn't half as good as the heroic dog stories everyone else had. So when my turn came I told Mrs. Israel that we had sheep in the basement. A mother named Licorice, because she was a black sheep (*where* was my therapist when I needed her most?), and her babies. Well, this story was a very big hit with the class and I went home to lunch and promptly forgot about it.

Especially because that day Mom was home from work, which was enough of a special occasion to make me forget school entirely. The phone rang and as I ate my peanut-butter-and-jelly sandwich I heard her tone grow progessively stern, then apologetic, then, oh boy, red alert. It seemed that it was Mrs. Israel calling. She wanted to arrange a field trip to our basement.

This was trouble like nobody's business now. I had to sit on the couch in the living room (a very bad sign) while Mom diagnosed me with "an overactive imagination." This did not seem a terribly desirable disease, especially when called by its other name, lying. Since I hadn't seen *Gypsy* yet, my idea was actually original. When I did, a few years later, I considered a lamb a perfectly logical gift.

I thought there was no one more beautiful than Natalie Wood, who played Gypsy Rose Lee, the famous stripper, no one more powerful than Rosalind Russell, who played her overbearing mother, and no one more terrifying than Baby June, Gypsy's younger sister. I don't remember the actress who played her. I do remember the perfect splits she did as the star of her vaudeville act, baton twirling and the little squeals of delight punctuating her every move. But what I remember most was her running away, at the age of thirteen, to get married.

She broke her mother's heart, which, of course, was the ultimate no-no. Though that wasn't the whole issue for me. I asked Mom a hundred questions. Where did she go? How did she get there? How can you get married when you're only junior high school age? And, by the way, why wasn't she ever in school? Most important, couldn't her mother find her and get her back?

Mom said that in some states at that time, you could get married at thirteen, but only with parental consent (she added that last part in case I had any ideas). She told me not to worry about Baby June because she grew up to be a famous actress named June Havoc. She would even point out her name in *TV Guide* when her films were on. Which only made me feel somewhat better. I actually knew Gypsy Rose Lee from *Hollywood Squares*. She seemed as funny and likeable and old as, say, Rose Marie. The notion of her taking off her clothes for anything but a bath seemed remote. But I could see her there, next to Paul Lynde and Wally Cox laughing away, being clever and cute and earnest all at the same time. June Havoc was not as easily found, starring in movies that were on too late for me to see or acting in plays in places too far away for me to go to.

In the movie of *Gypsy*, I identified with Natalie Wood, the no-talent striver relegated to the background while her dazzling sister headlined on the Orpheum Circuit at the age of seven. As a preteen girl myself, who despaired of ever attaining a trainer bra or a lipstick to call my own, the ugly-duckling-turned-swan story was close to my heart. But (big surprise) I also seemed to identify just as much with Rose, the mother. She worked and worked and did everything humanly possible to be a star. For her children to be stars.

Doesn't every child want to be a star? God knows I did. I wanted to do anything I saw on television. When I saw Mary Martin play Peter Pan I tried to fly off the dining-room table. When I saw *The Monkees* and the song over the the the credits said, "Anytime, anywhere, just look over your shoulder / guess who'll be standing there," I lurched around the house tossing my head every few minutes to see if it would happen. When it didn't, no one was more surprised than me.

So, I wanted both. I wanted to be the all-knowing, driving life force of Mama Rose and the happily-ever-after glamorous star Gypsy Rose Lee, who was photographed in the bath for *Vogue*. "I thought you did it for me, Mama," I would say in front of my mirror, trying to affect the same tones of disappointment and disdain Natalie Wood would summon for the line. And then I would slide to downright bitterness when, as Mama Rose, I would repeat, "I thought you did it for me, Mama. I thought you took a no-talent"—something or other—"and turned her into a star because you like doing things the hard way, Mama." I never could quite remember the words. Though I was a master at the resentment.

But where was June? I glimpsed her briefly during the mid-1980s in the crowded ladies' room of the Players Club, putting on red lipstick. She had a fabulous black pocketbook that looked French and worth a million bucks. I knew she was some sort of animal activist (the lambs ran in the family) and all the papers reported her doing good works for goats and gophers.

Years later, I met her. I was at a luncheon at the Marriott Marquis Hotel in honor of Jule Styne, who wrote the score to *Gypsy*, and someone pointed her out. She was sitting on the opposite side of the ballroom, wearing a big straw hat covered with flowers, and I approached, my heart beating wildly. She had no idea how happy I was to see her there in one piece. She looked quite well, actually, once I could focus on her face. Beautiful, in fact. I had spent so many childhood years worrying whether she had enough to eat, if she missed her mother, if she found a place to sleep each night. And here she was, just fine, thank you, wearing rouge and having chicken in the heart of Times Square.

I begged her for an interview. And though she looked at me rather oddly (who *was* this creature gripping her chair with that crazed look in her eye?), she agreed, and I went to her farm in Stamford, Connecticut, a few weeks later. She showed me her mementos of vaudeville, her pictures. She had a duckling in the backyard recuperating from some trauma or other, dropped off the day before by the ASPCA, and there were rabbits, dogs, cats, even a pig. After an hour or so she admitted she had been nervous about my coming. I admitted that I was nervous too. And when we were both done laughing, we were on our way to becoming friends.

After the article was published, we met for lunch a few times, just for fun. I had read both her books, *Early Havoc* and *More Havoc*, and I asked a ton of questions that she now felt free to answer since I wasn't writing about her anymore.

All along, she kept inviting me back to the farm, this time with Frank, who had left his job as drama critic to become a columnist for the *Times*'s op-ed page. He was safe, now. He couldn't review her. I also wanted to bring Mom (talk about the ultimate show-and-tell: look who I found!) and Phoebe too, who might appreciate better than anyone (except me) this woman whose legendary mother and sister had left their marks for life.

We decided on a picnic during the Fourth of July weekend, but I insisted on bringing the food. For a variety of reasons, including the fact that I was coming with two extra people. It's certainly not that Havoc, as she likes to be called, couldn't afford to entertain us. Quite the contrary. But her relationship to food is one I find as troubling as I do fascinating, habits born of a life lived on the road. I've seen her keep up an animated dinner conversation in a restaurant, all the while tucking rolls into a cloth napkin for her breakfast the next day. Without breaking eye contact she will pluck a doily off a saucer, separate it into three layers I never even knew it had and spear six balls of butter into it, to go with the bread. I've also seen her, in plain view, load up her pocketbook at opening-night buffets to bring dinner to her dogs. In *Early Havoc* she wrote of offending her brand-new mother-in-law by sitting at the woman's dinner table and automatically wiping down the silverware, since she had learned never to trust the cleanliness of her utensils.

To me, food has always been the basic pillar of home. I never had to look for it or plan for it. Three meals a day, every day, snacks not included. When I was away at school or traveling or any place that wasn't Mom's I would have specific cravings, either for her tuna fish or her meat loaf or her spaghetti with meat sauce. These foods *are* Mom, her love and support on a plate. I know that this is not altogether healthy either, but on the other hand food can be love much more easily than, for instance, sex. It's easier to get, for one thing. Food is a harbor, a refuge at the end of the day. To be surrounded by people you love, and given a huge pot of just about anything with garlic, well, you can die happy as far as I'm concerned.

"I used to get a dollar a day to eat no matter what, but I'm healthy," Havoc once told me. "Even though I would have lemon meringue pie for breakfast."

Inconceivable to me. First of all, that she would roam the streets at the age of seven or eight, seeking out food without even company, let alone supervision. Living in hotels and rooming houses and dressing rooms, never staying anywhere long, always moving on. But the stage was her sustenance. The applause. Every kid wants applause. That I could understand.

When the weekend arrived, Frank and I drove to Stamford separately from Mom and Phoebe, who got there first. Havoc seems most comfortable in a family of women; she doesn't have much curiosity about either my father or my brothers. I think the only reason she has any about Frank is because of the years he spent as a drama critic. She and Tana, her assistant, were out in the backyard underneath an enormous tree and Mom was having a cigarette, which I knew made Havoc insane but she was being perfectly polite about it.

Meanwhile, I took Tana inside to review the food. I had brought turkey and tuna-fish sandwiches, skinless fried chicken, a variety of pasta salads, brownies, fruit salad and too much of all of it. Which I learned from Mom. "Better too much than too little," she would always say. I loved it when she would entertain. No one could ever finish what she would put out. If my parents went to the movies with people and came back to our house for coffee that could also mean tuna fish or lox, bagels, a platter of cheeses, olives (but of course)—and that was *before* the cookies and cake. I would take the platters when they returned to the kitchen, barely touched, and sneak them upstairs.

Of course the flip side to all this food, this preoccupation with feeding, was that weight became an issue. I was never *fat* fat. At the worst it was twenty, twenty-five pounds overweight, which happened mostly in college when it was very fashionable to blame weight gain on your birth-control pills rather than visits to Dunkin' Donuts or the Norton House of Pizza, second home to the women of Wheaton. It specialized in something called a Hot Italian, which should have been a man but was an enormous hero sandwich filled with cold cuts, topped with melted provolone. Unlike a man, it really stayed with you.

Then I went through a period of flirting with bulimia, equally as fashionable, I might add, at a women's college. (Tip to the uninitiated: Always end a meal with ice cream. It comes up easily.)

Finally, it was exercise that controlled my weight best. Until my ankle, of course. Why am I always so extreme? I overdo everything. Including the volume of food I brought today, but I know that if no one else could finish it, the dogs could.

Back under the tree the conversation progressed as Tana and I presented the food. "Oh, our kosher picnic!" cried Havoc, tickled by my catering complex. Of course it wasn't kosher at all, but just as I was enraptured by her life in vaudeville, she was enraptured by my life in kosher.

"Everyone did everything for Mother," Havoc said, as we all sat down. "She was rather helpless—little, blue-eyed, with soft curling hair and a sweet, endearing personality." This was certainly hard to imagine, considering the women who've played her. Ethel Merman, Rosalind Russell, Tyne Daly.

"She died about 1956," Havoc said. "She was about fifty-seven."

Uh-oh. I was born in 1957. Maybe she was reincarnated as me. Help! No wonder I'm obsessed with her family.

Havoc was first onstage at the age of two, billed as Dainty June Hovick, the Toe Dancer. It turned out she never even went to school. "I learned to read by sound," she said. "With the Oz books and the Bibles in the hotel rooms. I was awfully ashamed of that, until I was a completely grown-up person."

"When we played Rochester," she recalled, "the birth certificate made me sixteen years old when I was really about nine. They stopped the act, pulled me off the stage and sent me to the shelter. I had no molars yet, so how could I be sixteen without molars? They were going to take me away from Mother. I wandered around town alone, no education, no thought of it. I looked well. I was delighted to be on the stage, who wouldn't be? I did three or four shows a day, even when I was sick. I had chicken pox, mumps and measles, but Mother took care of me as best she could." She added that she did not work at all when she had German measles. "I had to sit in a dark room, 'cause you could go blind in the light."

Where was her father through all this? "As soon as I got up on my toes Mother left him," she said. "I was eighteen months old and didn't even talk yet. Gypsy was four years older than me and went to school. When she joined the act she was billed as Rose Louise, the Doll Girl. By the time I was two, I was appearing around Seattle. I was an escape.

"When I did my first film in Hollywood," she continued, "my sister said 'our father wants to see you.' So, I took my friend, the actor Sam Levene, to dinner with me. We sat through it and Sammy went to get the car and my father said, 'You don't want to be seen with him,

June, he's a Jew.' That was my own father and I thought, 'I don't know you at all and I don't care if I do or not,' and never saw him again.'"

Mom had had her tight mouth going since the part about the German measles and Phoebe was looking at Havoc as if she'd just landed from outer space. I looked at her and wondered how she had survived with any sense of self at all, with a mother who adored her only on stage.

After Havoc ran away, she and her sixteen-year-old husband joined the dance marathon circuit. Her descriptions of it in her books were harrowing: being allowed to sleep only thirty minutes every twelve hours. But they were fed regularly, which she hadn't been after leaving her mom. This was a woman who knew what it meant to go hungry; not only that, but to go hungry as a has-been at the age of thirteen. When vaudeville was dying and Havoc wanted to leave it to become a stage actress, her mother refused. She loved her daughter's stardom. Why waste time or money on theater training? Any signs to the contrary, vaudeville would surely last forever. Years later, Havoc wrote, when she moved back to live with her mother in New York City, she was charged for meals.

I looked around me, at her beautiful farm. She has Tana, who is like a daughter. (Her own daughter, April, lives in France and is rarely mentioned.) She had two husbands after the first one and she still speaks quite affectionately about the last, who died years ago. Her animals are everywhere and she loves them. And the scrapbooks are inside, filled with decades of the work she has never stopped and has no intention of stopping. Okay. She wasn't raised in a house with homework and tuna fish. Her source of nurture was just different from mine. It didn't mean she doesn't have any.

Havoc wanted seconds of everything. What I admire about her— being something like eighty-two (with all the phony birth certificates, nothing is certain)—is that she eats with a real appetite. She's gotten a little frail (she tripped and fell running after one of the animals and broke twenty-two bones in her feet a few years ago) but she has a tremendous life force. Three weeks after she broke her feet, she co-starred in *Love Letters* with Van Johnson on Martha's Vineyard. In a wheelchair.

"Vaudeville wouldn't even eat in the same restaurants or stay in the same hotels as burlesque," she was saying now. "There really were classes of people. And vaudeville was very proud, extremely proud. In *Gypsy,* burlesque was all cutified, not the way it really was, down and dirty, men with raw liver and milk bottles masturbating. That was the audience.

"Gypsy was fifteen years old when she started. She saw the other women doing it and said, 'They're starring, I can do that.' One of the earliest times I caught my sister stripping in Bedford, Mass., I was on my way back from a marathon. I went in and didn't know if I should go backstage, because this was not the elegant act she became famous for later. It was a way to start. I did go backstage and that's when she told me, 'You should see what they sweep out of here every night, June.' She drank a lot of gin, because it was against her grain to do what she did. But she was determined to get out of a hole."

I remembered a conversation then I had had with Havoc at one of our lunches, when we were discussing my fixation on her life. It seemed hard for her to fathom that we could have anything in common. "Your life is such a pillow," she had said. I thought about that for a long time. Because in spite of our apparent differences, she just didn't feel that foreign to me.

Maybe what we had in common was the urge to please. The willingness to perform onstage or off, eager to be loved for doing something right, or better than any other child could. I think we also had in common the urge for flight, only she acted on it. And she always wanted to improve herself, learn her craft better, learn about people, see things no one else could see, which helped her as an actress. For me, the urge was to try to be a writer. She was right about the pillow, the Scarsdale life of maids and Mom's credit cards to buffer the blows, but nonetheless our insides didn't seem so terribly different.

And while her sister would do anything to succeed and dignity be damned—what else can you call stripping when you get right down to it, no matter how elegant the presentation?—she was clearly conflicted about it. The price and the prize didn't always jibe. Not with Havoc, though. Maybe she was never as big a star as Gypsy, but her values lined up right behind to support her, never to knock her off balance and make her fall.

"Gypsy was always trying to educate me, to brighten me up," Havoc said. "You've got to learn how to crap the crappers because I do."

"But you were talented," Mom protested.

"Talent didn't matter to anybody; she felt terribly sorry for me," Havoc said. "She would try to give me clothes and money. And Mother didn't even think about me anymore 'cause I was a loser. 'We never expected you to surface,' she said when I came back after the marathons. I was gawky, no great beauty. I never had a plan. Gypsy created a creature that was a real shocker. But it was her wit and natural intelligence, it never would have worked without it. She was brilliant."

She had tears in her eyes at the memory. She missed her sister.

"Once Gypsy went to the Metropolitan Opera wearing a cape of orchids down to the floor. She always wanted to be noticed, while it was my dream not to be seen. I just wanted to see. It's a different chemical thing with an actor."

This made sense to me. I always had a hard time being noticed. What if something was wrong? Not Phoebe. When she was fifteen she and her friend, who lived next door, took it upon themselves to go to Studio 54. (Mom would have *killed* her, had she known. Once again, she only found out after the fact.) Phoebe put on her friend's mother's dress, an Oscar de la Renta silk taffeta gown complete with crinoline, and a ton of makeup and off they went. And got in. Happy to be a fairy princess at a moment's notice. All I could do if I ever even got that far would be to obsess about midnight. And getting the heel of the glass slipper caught in the hem of the dress. Which Phoebe did, actually. She got the heel caught, fell and ripped the crinoline. And went home, put it right back into the cleaner's plastic in the woman's closet and never thought about it again. A cape of orchids? Why not?

The sky was overcast, so we moved indoors, sat at the round dining-room table and started on the scrapbooks. Which were astonishing.

One shot of Havoc showed her on a billboard a block long above the Winter Garden theater on Broadway when she starred in *Mexican Hayride* in 1944.

"You were pre–Calvin Klein," Phoebe said admiringly.

There were pictures of marquees emblazoned with "Dainty June" in every city imaginable. "Demoines Theater," one caption read in her mother's handwriting. "Bad city labor law, June unable to finish," she wrote. In Sioux City, it read, "June stopping both Sunday shows, poor house Monday." In Omaha, "No electric sign in front, bad city, labor laws."

Where was Herbie, the character from *Gypsy* who managed the act? "That was Murray Gordon," Havoc said. "He was an observant Jew and he used to pray every night with my hat on from the act. I loved him. We never used a toothbrush or went to the dentist before him."

What happened? "Mother killed him," she said sternly. "She didn't love him enough. He wanted me to have training, a future. And Mother was happy to settle for the present. I was out there killing the people, what more could you want? Finally, she told him, 'We don't need you.' I remember him kneeling at the bathtub washing our dirty laundry. It was so sad.

"Mama never knew the difference between rayon and silk," she went on angrily. "Gordon stayed till I was eleven. He could see no future, nothing."

She shook herself upright. "I don't believe in being marked as a child because someone dropped your baby spoon," she said crisply. "I would be a rapist or murderer at this point, given my background, if that were true."

I suddenly wanted to go outside. The room felt dark and close and I wanted air. I'd had enough of this mother who ran her daughters all over the country to please herself, who denied them the dignity of even a rudimentary education, who would only allow her "baby" to miss a show if she might go blind and jeopardize the act.

I told Tana I wanted to see Homer, the pig, whom I had missed last time. We went out back and she made some clucking noises and he appeared from behind a fence. This was a pig? He looked like a building. I had no idea a pig could be so huge. I leaned down to look into his eyes. He looked back, clear, calm, dare I say smart? There was a person in there!

"Look," I told Phoebe. "Look into his eyes. There's someone in there. Maybe he's being punished from his last life for eating too much."

But she had a better idea. She wanted to feed me to Homer.

"What are you doing?" I asked as she pushed me toward him.

"Look, he's hungry," she said, teeth gleaming. "Go on. Get in there."

I could see that after a day of discussing an overpowering sister, Phoebe had had it. The past few months had been a time of upheaval for her, anyway. She had left the Pace Gallery right after our trip to find Leona Helmsley and since then had been trying to get work on a film crew as a set decorator. To pay her rent she became a hostess at a Mexican restaurant in Midtown. Finally, finally, she was hired for an independent feature film that would start shooting two days from now. She could stay in New York and she was thrilled. Not to mention terrified. So feeding me to Homer seemed as good a diversion as any.

She pushed me again.

"Mommy! Phoebe's trying to feed me to the pig."

Mom looked up from her conversation with Tana with the glint of an eye that has tamed me for a lifetime.

I turned back to Phoebe. "I hate you," I said.

"Why?" Phoebe acted injured. "The pig looks hungry. I was just trying to help him."

It was time to leave, and not one moment too soon considering that Phoebe had really caught Homer's attention. He seemed to emit an air of great expectation.

We said all our good-byes, and Frank and I drove to see some friends nearby, where we were going to spend the night. From their den, I called Mom and Phoebe at home.

Phoebe answered. "Hi," I said. "Let me talk to Mommy."

"She's making lamb chops, she can't talk to you now," she said. "Why wouldn't you let me feed you to the pig?"

"Ha-ha. What did you think of Havoc?"

"I really liked her," she said. "She's so kind, she doesn't say anything bad about anyone. I think she had a really hard life. She kept saying, 'Who wouldn't love being onstage,' but I think that was drummed into her by her mother. I really wanted to ask her, was she scared when she left at thirteen, being so young? Was she that driven for her career?"

"Why didn't you ask, then?"

"I just didn't feel comfortable enough. I think she must be a very free spirit. People like that amaze me. To leave her family and everything familiar. It's sort of incredible."

The extension picked up.

"Hello, sweetheart," Mom said.

"I thought she was making lamb chops and couldn't speak to me, Phoebe."

"Ha-ha," she said.

"Mommy, Phoebe tried to feed me to the pig."

"Stop it, already, the two of you."

Phoebe hung up.

"I thought she was marvelous," Mom said. "She was very generous in her hospitality and so was Tana. June has been bounced around so much and still speaks about people in such generous terms. Even though she was different from her sister, she's not that different. Her sister knew what she wanted and went after it. June knew she had to get away and she did. But those years of struggling must have been disastrous."

We talked some more and then it was time for her to turn the lamb chops, so she had to get off. I hung up the phone and sat at our friend's desk in his beautiful country house and listened to my husband outside, talking to him, while his wife was in the kitchen making comforting noises, like ripping sheets of Reynolds Wrap out of the box for a barbecue while the smell of a freshly baked peach pie floated through the house.

Havoc would call this a pillow and she would be right, of course. I walked back into the kitchen, offering to carry the drinks outside. As we talked about the day and the air got cooler and our legs started to get bitten, the coals glowed and sausages went on the grill. Why was I just not in the mood? Because they could be Homer?

I thought about Mom's lamb chops, sprinkled with garlic powder and Lawry's Seasoned Salt, cooked until they're charred around the edges. She probably made broccoli with them and because time was short, Heinz baked beans, to which she added ketchup and chili sauce, which makes them extra delicious. And when they were finished eating and Mom had loaded the dishwasher they would sit outside on the deck and she'd have her cigarette. And after they'd moved inside, Mom to the black chair, Phoebe to the green couch, they'd talk about the day. About Havoc and her mother and her sister. And Mom would say, "You see how lucky you are?"

And Phoebe would nod and kiss her and hug her and then they'd start to watch a movie before Mom would say, "I have to go upstairs now and wash my head," which she always said instead of hair. And Phoebe would say, "No, Mommy, don't go," because she didn't want to be downstairs alone for half an hour. But Mom would go anyway and come down smelling of Dial soap and a clean, fresh nightgown with her hair pulled back and her wide cheekbones gleaming with moisturizer. And then they'd finish watching the movie and talk some more and Mom would make little packages of her cigarette butts in a napkin before she threw them out so the garbage wouldn't smell, and then she'd check to see that the front door was locked and the two of them would head up the stairs together, to bed.

I felt better, I realized. I was even getting some appetite. The pillow Havoc was talking about, I saw finally, wasn't just money or things. It was family. The soft, protected place to come to at the end of a day, to hug, to cry into, to lean on.

And I knew that mine was tucked in for the night. I could relax.

chapter seven

Once a Mommy

We moved into the house on Myrtledale Road in the fall of 1969. Twenty-five years later my parents moved out, a day I thought would never come. From the very first time we all drove to the swampy-looking plot on which it was built, I have thought of that house as home.

Before we moved there, we lived a few other places, all in Passaic, New Jersey. The first was Barry Gardens, an apartment complex I remember only dimly, since we left when I was three. I have two recollections of it, both involving television. The first was being walked up and down the length of the living room by Dad while *Perry Mason* was on and Mom was passed out in the bedroom from the exhaustion of teaching and studying for her PhD at the same time. The goal of this walking was to get me to do the same. Why anyone thought that constant movement was a way to put children to sleep is a mystery, but so were most conventions of the 1950s. Who wanted to sleep? It was like being on a ride. The other thing I remember was learning the twist from Chubby Checker, who was a lot more fun than Perry Mason.

Then came the house on Terhune Avenue. Greg was born while we lived there. It had a backyard and a garden and a big tree that was slanted enough to climb. And it was then that President Kennedy was assassinated. I was six at the time, in first grade, and that day we were rehearsing our Thanksgiving pageant. Half the class were Pilgrims, the other half Indians. We had the kind of classroom door that had a small window in the middle, and as the Pilgrims' dinner preparations were getting under way (I don't know what the Indians were doing, but they all had cardboard tomahawks) a janitor looked through and Mrs. Israel went out to talk to him. When she came back she was crying.

I had never seen a teacher cry. For that matter, I hadn't seen many grown-ups cry. And she absolutely wept. The Pilgrims stopped assembling their cornucopias and the Indians put down the maize they had made out of construction paper and the principal came on the loudspeaker and ordered everyone to observe a minute of silence.

When I got home, I found more tears from Mom, and the enormity of the situation finally sank in. You see, back in the days before she went blonde, Mom's hair was as jet black as Grandma's, and like most women of her generation she seemed to bear an uncanny resemblance to Jackie Kennedy. The coats, the hats, and in my mother's case, the cheekbones. I also knew that I was Caroline's age, and Greg was John-John's. So I figured out that this meant my father was about to be killed. (Isn't it remarkable how, when you're a child, every world event seems to happen to you and you alone? And isn't it even more remarkable that no matter how old you get that doesn't ever change?)

After a few years had passed and, miraculously, my father wasn't killed, we moved to the house on Ridge Avenue. This is where we were when Phoebe was born. This is also where Greg and I got into some real trouble. One Sunday, Mom and Dad went somewhere and we stayed home, probably to play with the kids next door, the Kimmels, which really meant going into their basement to peruse their father's extensive collection of *Playboy* magazines. Somehow, though, probably because their parents were home that day, we ended up playing outside and managed to lock ourselves out of the house.

We contemplated the front door for a while before I had the ingenious notion of picking the lock. I was ten at the time and I'm sure I heard this term in a James Cagney movie, but I somehow translated it as taking a pair of scissors, sticking one blade into the lock and turning. The blade broke right off. In retrospect, I learned that this was jamming, not picking. Well, I was dumbfounded. Somehow my monumental grasp of physics had not allowed for this possibility.

By the time my parents got home, I had cooked up some sensational story about what happened, but it didn't work at all. (They got in, no problem, with the electric remote for the garage door.) After a few calls, it was determined the locksmith couldn't come until Monday, and not only that but *it was going to cost $25*, an apparently princely sum. Mom took Greg into his room and Dad took me into my room to mete out the punishment, and while I'm not sure what the psychosexual implications of this gender split were, I can tell you that it hurt like a sonofabitch. I can also tell you the thought crossed my mind that if my father had been assassinated after all, I would have been able to sit down that night. But alas . . .

After Ridge Avenue came the Carlton Towers, a high-rise apartment building where we lived while waiting for the house in Scarsdale to be built. I liked the Carlton Towers, with its nighttime views of city lights and its outdoor swimming pool. I do remember, though, some mishaps that occurred while we lived there, probably because it was a time of change, of turmoil, of storage. Who can concentrate properly on life when separated from their tchotchkes?

Two things happened to Mom. The first was when she was trying to push a cart of groceries up a ramp into the building's service entrance but the wheels got caught somehow and it turned over, knocking her down and landing on her leg. As she lay underneath it trying to get up, I did the only heroic thing a firstborn daughter and leader of women could do. Fainted dead away. I couldn't begin to watch this. I woke up in the elevator, being carried by Dad. After languishing in bed awhile and finding out that Mom was just fine, I was too.

The second thing that happened was much worse. As we know, Mom was always trying to do too much. At this point in her life she had three kids, one an infant and all living in temporary housing, a full-time job *and* she was president of the Passaic Board of Education. And in 1969 that meant phone calls at all hours of the day and night about riots and protests and vandalism. But in the midst of it all, she decided to actually listen to Greg and me when we complained about how boring it was to have peanut butter and jelly for lunch *again*.

So one day we came home to find Mom in residence, starting to fry an impressive array of hors d'oeuvres, things like pigs in blankets, potato knishes, kreplach. We were beside ourselves with anticipation. Then, in her usual rush, she managed to tip the pan of hot oil onto her hand. This was an unspeakable sight. She started to curse (very out of character) while doubled up over the sink, her red hand curled under a stream of cold water. When I made the mistake of asking how she was, she started to yell and told me to take care of my own goddamned lunch. Which was, you guessed it, peanut butter and jelly. And if we thought it was crummy when Mom made it, we just hadn't lived until I tried it.

Finally, the house on Myrtledale Road was finished and we moved in. Emmett was born. But there were only four bedrooms, one for my parents and three for the rest of us. Phoebe and I were roommates in the biggest bedroom, Greg had his own, and Emmett, of course, needed the remaining one for a nursery. So there we were, me and

Phoebe, twelve years old and two years old, in the same room. Talk about the odd couple. A year later it switched, and I got my own room while Phoebe and Emmett shared. Then Greg went in with Emmett and Phoebe took his room, which she never gave up, especially after she had the walls tattooed.

I knew that house by heart. If I was blindfolded, I could tell exactly where I was by the feel of the room, its sound and smell. Each had its own. First there was the foyer. When I stayed out all night during the summers and came back at dawn, no place was more welcoming. The wooden floors smelled of lemon polish, there were roses from Mom's garden on the front-hall table and the central air-conditioning was on. That had its own smell, clean, calming. With a little bit of a hum. To the right was the living room. When we were small, the furniture was covered in plastic. Greg volunteered the theory that in addition to being allergic to dogs and cats, our parents were allergic to us.

The living room was for special occasions. And piano lessons, such as they were. Poor Mr. Wasserman, the most beleaguered piano teacher in Scarsdale. I never practiced. So we quickly gave up on classics like "Für Elise" and tried for something contemporary like "The Green Berets." With a beat. At the opposite end of the room from the piano was a huge mirror Mom found at an estate sale. I spent my entire adolescence comparing how fat my legs looked in that mirror to how fat they looked in the front-hall mirror, and finally declared the living-room mirror the winner because there they always looked thinner. Maybe it was the light.

A door led from the living room to the den, where the green couch and the black chair lived. Not to mention the fireplace. And the encyclopedia, which Dad would read the way other people read magazines. I don't know if he figured that his kids brought home such a paltry number of research projects that he hadn't gotten his money's worth, or that he just wanted to know things (both, I think), but there he would be, down on the floor reading a volume whenever you looked. (Mom used to read the dictionary, just for fun. Is this a pair, or what?)

Then there was the guest bathroom, where Grandma showed me all the shapes in the wallpaper. And where, in eighth grade, I wept my way through *Love Story*.

Next to that was the kitchen. Holy of holies, center of the house. A perfect place except for the lack of a second oven, a terrible hardship that Mom remembered to complain about three times a year on holidays. (Hence the hot trays.) There were also her piles. She would make piles out of bills, mailings, any piece of paper would do on the telephone table, and they would stack up until Dad complained and then there would be one marathon day when she would attack the piles and they would disappear. Until three days later when they miraculously grew back.

Off the kitchen was the laundry room and the maid's room with bathroom, where Greg thought he was sneaking in through the garage one night at 3:00 A.M., only to find Mom in there reading *Passages*. That's when we decided she was in menopause for sure. The fact that she would come home from work, say hello, and drop her clothes as she walked through the house should have been something of a clue. "Why is it so *hot*?" she would ask, stepping out of her shoes and dropping her jacket. Then she would unbutton her shirt and unzip her skirt, still walking, doing whatever it was she would normally do, leaving little piles on the floor to match the ones near the phone. It was just weird enough to be Mom. But *Passages*! Aha! We finally figured it out.

Next to the kitchen was the dining room. The mark on the ceiling still remained from a champagne cork that got away during a seder or a Thanksgiving dinner, any holiday that wasn't New Year's when Dad would open a bottle and say, "Happy New Year," anyway.

Near the stairs to the second floor, in the foyer, was the statue. This thing was the bane of my existence from the minute Dad found it in someone else's closet—bound for the junk heap, no doubt—though he considered it high art. The statue was a guy holding up a cluster of grapes, which unfortunately echoed his exposed crotch. Somewhere in his travels, he had been trimmed of his manhood. Which was just the kind of welcome you want to give a date coming through the door to pick you up.

As the kids got older, the statue proved potentially hazardous, which was worse than embarrassing. If you had too much to drink, or were coming in past curfew, trying to keep quiet, the statue was positioned in such a way that you had to remember to walk two extra steps to the right in the dark on the way upstairs or the damn thing could topple over. We all had our close calls, with it rocking perilously on its pedestal, but (unfortunately) it managed to endure.

Upstairs, the large bedroom Phoebe and I had started out sharing had gone to Emmett. One time when Mom and Dad were out and Emmett and I were home alone, we decided to violate the kosher rule and order in some baked ziti from the pizza place. No sooner was it delivered and we were removing the plastic forks from the bag, than they came home. Shit! We flew up to Emmett's room and hid it in his closet until we could bring it downstairs to the garage and devour it.

Then came the bedroom that had been mine. It was connected to the unheated storeroom and was colder than any room in the house. I was convinced that this was done deliberately, to ruin my life, certainly my teenage life, and maybe even stunt my growth. If Phoebe had had the cold room, she wouldn't be five inches taller than me.

But she had the room next door, nice and cozy, with its wall-to-wall violet shag rug. Then there was the kids' bathroom with the leaky shower and a perpetual line out the door, and my parents' room. Aside from Mom's closet and jewelry drawer ("Can I borrow . . . ?") we didn't spent much time in there.

When Mom and Dad said they'd put the house up for sale, I didn't really believe them. I figured the real estate market was terrible and no one would buy it. Which was true for almost two years. But after that really bad winter with the seventeen snowstorms, Dad had had enough. He didn't want to shovel the drive anymore. Or clean the rain gutters. Or call when the air-conditioning broke. Again.

All of a sudden it seemed to just happen. Someone bid enough and they accepted. The only problem was that they had nowhere to go. A big part of this was because Mom didn't want to move. She hates change even more than I do. So the Queen of Passive Aggression would say, "Oh, yes, let's look at apartments, by all means, but I have a class to prepare, or a budget to prepare, or a beef stew to prepare and I don't have time right now."

Finally, they found an apartment in Scarsdale Village, an enclave of tradition and quaintness, with the recent and rude exception of a Dunkin' Donuts. So déclassé.

They moved in August 1994. This was no small feat after twenty-five years of accumulating stuff, not just ours but everyone else's. Grandma's entire apartment was in our basement, for starters. Not to mention camp trunks, college notebooks (thank God I saved the one on Chaucer, which has proved truly indispensable in real life), Ping-Pong tables, patio furniture. A total mess.

And I could see Mom was starting to bug out. She never had time (read: made time) to pack. Or go through things and keep or throw them away. The kids did it all in spurts, when we were there. Then, finally, it was really happening, and she had to deal with it. And right on schedule, of course, she did.

But here they were, at the last minute, moving into an apartment that hadn't been touched in thirty years. For all the usual boring reasons surrounding a co-op, it took forever to close, so there was no time to fix it. The good part was how big it was, but it was also unpainted, with stained carpet, and dark as night, with about four electrical outlets.

Couldn't they just stay in a hotel while it was worked on? Apparently not. The High Holidays fell on Labor Day that year and there they were. Phoebe and I decided to go up on Kol Nidre night, the night before Yom Kippur, and sleep over. Then everyone could come into the city to my apartment to break the fast since, obviously, Mom couldn't entertain amid boxes in the dark.

When we got to the apartment, a number of things disturbed me. First of all, Mom. She seemed to be doing everything right, but nothing felt right. She boiled the chicken in the same salt-free way she always boiled it, so no one would get thirsty during the fast. She underseasoned the soup for the same reason. We broke off a piece of challah and Dad said a prayer and we dipped it into honey so that we would all have a sweet year. (Since Frank was not there, I was doing this on his behalf too. Observant Jew that he is, he said, "Pray for me, honey," kissed me good-bye, and went to dinner with a friend, for ribs.)

But Mom's heart just wasn't in it. Boxes lay everywhere (including one containing that damn statue) and rugs were rolled up and stacked against the walls. It occurred to me that the problem here was children. Or lack thereof. When Mom had to make a home for her children, her efforts were tireless. There were packers and movers and deliveries of space-age washing machines and dishwashers by the minute. But this time it was just for her. And Dad. It wasn't the same. Sure, they had a guest room. And they had ordered a pull-out couch for the den, since Mom had given the green couch to Greg, who needed furniture. (You can imagine how well that went over with the rest of us. Phoebe goes to his apartment now just to visit the couch.)

The children had always been the focus of our family. Not a brilliant revelation, but suddenly so clear. Everything had been for our education, our upbringing, our safety, our welfare. And our parents had succeeded so well that we were all gone. Now what?

Of course, that was not an issue I could comfortably discuss with

Mom. I was thirty-seven and childless and she had had quite enough of me. When I (*finally*) got married at thirty-three, I think she and Dad figured I would make up for lost time and start breeding immediately. The problem was that I seemed to be the only one who didn't hear my biological clock ticking. I just didn't have this overwhelming *need* that so many women I know seem to have, where they must have a child or die. Their relationship with their husbands isn't as important. Their relationship with their work isn't as important. They simply must have a child this very minute.

And it seems to have worked out quite well for all of them, since each one has a genuis. Or two. Not only that, but with creative talent so extraordinary it could only be compared to, say, Wolfgang Amadeus Mozart. (There's the perfect reason right there for me not to have children. I would probably just have a baby.)

Of course, when it came down to it, I felt that I had already had babies. Phoebe. Emmett. Mom. Yes. It wasn't easy for her to be Super-Mom all those years and who better to help her than me? I was bright and capable, as she always told me. So I gave bottles, played peekaboo, changed diapers, drove the paper route in the rain, cooked dinner, packed the lunches.

And now that every woman I know wants to ditch nine-to-five to learn the alphabet from scratch, I just shrug. Done that, been there. I was actually under the impression, now that everyone else had grown up, I might get to be the child for a change and explore what interests *me*. There's a concept. Do what I want to do instead of what I'm supposed to do.

In my particular situation, I married a man and his two children, and I knew that going in. As a matter of fact, at our wedding, after Frank and I fed each other the cake, I fed a piece to Nat and a piece to Simon. I made a commitment to being a stepmother, and not the kind Cinderella had. This notion is one almost no one feels comfortable with. Most of the stepmothers I know, and, I should add, all of whom are older than me, propagate a stance of "us" versus "them." *Us* means the biological children they have with their husband. *Them* means the ones he had before they got there.

I am not comfortable with this. First of all, I really like my step-kids. When we first met, they were ten and five. Now they are fifteen and eleven. From the beginning I have found them both extraordinarily kind, smart, funny, sensitive, interesting and interested in everything in the world around them. So, okay, Wolfgang Amadeus may have been some guy, but he was nothing compared to these kids. I'm as guilty as the rest.

The question, to me at least, then becomes, why do I need another one? So it would be mine? Meaning what, exactly? How "mine" is any child, ultimately? How "mine" are we to my parents, sitting here now in the dark emptiness of a strange place they don't know how to fill up without the aid of cribs and playpens and strollers? Shouldn't this all-consuming love so many women seem to be looking for be gotten from another like-minded adult who can reciprocate, rather than by a child biologically programmed for abandonment?

I look at Nat and Simon and find them irresistible. Thanks to my training as a surrogate mother, I help with homework, bake last-minute brownies for the bake sale and put Band-Aids on boo-boos with great aplomb. I yell about teeth being brushed and hair being washed, and I remind them each ten times to throw away their tissues once they've blown their noses into them, because I am not going to do it for them.

"What does your mother do when you leave these around?" I asked Nat recently. He didn't blink. "She picks them up," he said. "Well, she loves you more than I do," I replied. And I'm sure she does. But I still think that instead of writing off my relationship to them as unbiological and therefore somehow invalid, another look should be taken at the alternatives.

What if I just became a terrific stepmother without trying to produce my very own genetic genius? Would that be so bad? Has there ever been a child in the history of the world whose life was ruined because too many people loved him? I don't think so.

When I was growing up, and sometimes still, if the truth be told, I wanted a real-life fairy godmother, an Auntie Mame, just with a functioning sense of reality. Where was that extra person who could step in when neither parent would do? Because they don't always. Especially as kids get older and you start to see parents' limitations. You don't stop loving them. You just look for something extra. Why not be that something extra? Having children is really a display of astonishing ego, when you stop to think about it. And the joke is so often on the parents, because they don't get what they expect. They forget that these children are people, separate people with their own personalities from the start. Mom always said that each of us exhibited a personality from day one, and it was uncannily similar to how we eventually turned out. Kids are not just little blank slates waiting to be filled up with Mom or Dad's agenda.

Being a stepparent, of course, is even more of a thankless job than being a parent. First of all, you are always the third choice. No matter how much they like you, no one considers you an option for anything until Mom and Dad are unavailable first. And though that's normal, the temptation is to push, to try to be just as important. But then they get confused, because, at a young age especially, there's a loyalty issue, and they don't want to feel they're betraying their mother if they actually end up liking you. You have to be careful with the "I love you"s. You have to show that, more than say it, or you force them to reciprocate out loud, and realizing that yes, they do love you too, might be more information than they really need to know. So the deal is to keep giving and understand that you're the last one on the thank-you list. You're taken for granted because you can't be taken too seriously.

You certainly learn patience this way, which for me is the ultimate lesson. I know that when the kids are grown up and can understand the subtleties, our relationships will bloom in ways they can't now. For the present, it's enough to hear Simon call excitedly, "Alex, Alex, watch this, I want to show you something!" his face lit with the anticipation of my reaction. To see Nat walking ahead of me with Frank and Simon, as they so often did when my ankle was slowing me down, and watch him turn and look for me. Frank didn't. But Nat kept an eye out for me, seeing that I crossed the street okay, went down the stairs to the right subway platform. These are the sweet moments, the unspoken "I love you"s of stepchildren.

And now that we're moving into their teenage years, I feel the advantage is definitely shifting. When no one is more loathsome than your parents, stepparents can look semi-loathsome by comparison. That step can work both ways.

So, Mom's argument then goes, if I'm such a fount of love, why not have even more children?

And you know why? Because I can't do everything. I have worked my entire life to deny it, but it's true. Unlike Wonder Woman—my mother, Barbara Witchel—I simply cannot do everything. I can't have a full-time career as a writer and an absorbing marriage and a fulfilling stepmotherhood and at almost forty (because who knows how long it would take to even get pregnant now) have a baby. And let the work slide and the husband slide and the stepkids slide. I don't want to.

I was having dinner recently with some women I know and shared a cab home with two of them. One is my age. She got pregnant the morning after her wedding and her life has been a roller coaster of baby, marriage and freelance work for both her and her husband ever since. The other woman is forty-three, divorced, and the mother of two adopted boys, five and two. We were all talking about fatigue, of course, and I was trying to explain why I was so tired. Working full-time at the paper, trying to write a book, having the kids every weekend. The woman with adopted children nodded reassuringly. "You're doing so much," she said soothingly. "It's hard."

But the other woman, my friend, whom I have known for years, just laughed. "I can't listen to anyone without kids say they're exhausted," she said dismissively.

"But she does have them, just part-time," the adoptive mother said.

"That doesn't count," the other declared.

Now, this is one of those moments when all your years of therapy tell you that instead of strangling your dear friend, you must silently remind yourself that this is her problem, not yours, that she has anger about things you don't know about and on and on. While trying not to seethe. And when I was done trying not to seethe because I was seething anyway, I decided, fuck it. You really can't have it all and you do have to choose. I chose what I have and she chose what she has, failed diaphragm notwithstanding. Someone feels she's better than me? I'm sure she's right. As the biological, full-time mother of a child, she is nobility and as the unbiological part-time mother, I am shit. And you know what? I still choose what I have and just that. Not more. Not other.

Thankfully, Yom Kippur is not one of those child-focused holidays, so no one now was particularly pining for the kids, the way they do if they miss a seder. Once the tasteless chicken dinner was finished and we all went to temple and came back, Phoebe and I changed into our nightgowns. We couldn't watch TV because it was Yom Kippur and television wasn't allowed. Probably one of those hidden passages in Genesis knew in advance that television would be invented and no one should watch it. We decided to go out on the terrace, a cute little one off the living room, where we could smoke without Dad smelling it. Because God will also forgive you quicker on Yom Kippur if He can't smell tobacco on your breath. (Exodus?)

What did we talk about? The new neighbors, the laundry room, everything except what we should have been talking about. Like why Mom hadn't wanted to move out of the house, even though she said she did. Like why she didn't want to move in here, because maybe it meant she was getting old and the world was getting smaller and that scared her. Like why she didn't approve of my not wanting to have children, even though she'd never intended to have any herself, back when she was a budding biochemist.

Are children just not enough, in the end? Maybe the same limits kids find with their parents work both ways. The biggest problem for children and adults, as Auntie Mame's nephew discovered, is when you become an adult yourself you find that your parents are just as fallible as you are. And who wants to know that? It's much more reassuring for everyone when parents are magical. They certainly don't get to be outside the house. So, once their children grow up, yes, love and respect should remain on both sides. But magic? Superhuman powers? For that, you need grandchildren.

And while Nat and Simon fill something of Mom's grandmotherly needs, they don't quite do the trick. They found her too late. She still enjoys them, though, because they're great kids. And because they're mine. There's enough of that trace of magic left between us as parent and child that means as long as something is mine, is something I do or something I care about, she will embrace it. Once a mommy, always a mommy. And her doing so is of paramount importance to me. Once a daughter, always a daughter.

As for Phoebe, Nat thinks she's cool, certainly cooler than his dad or me, since she actually watches MTV for more than scientific purposes and knows the groups he talks about. She gets along well with Simon too, but I think that, like Mom, she would have preferred the baby part right from the start. For me, the older they are, the more interesting they become.

Later in the evening, after Mom went to bed, Phoebe and I talked awhile in the dark. It was quiet here, at least. She fell asleep first, after turning over and over. She sounded like a cement mixer. I fell asleep too, finally, but when I woke up, I couldn't imagine where I was. Some storeroom I had never seen, filled with things from our house.

Phoebe looked over at me. "Hi," she said.

"Hi," I answered. "Um, excuse me. Could you possibly tell me where we are?"

"Yeah, really," she said, pulling herself out of bed and beating me to the bathroom.

I went outside to find Mom rummaging through a closet. "I can't find what I want to wear," she said. "I don't remember where I put it."

Dad, of course, was already gone. We were supposed to meet him at temple, or rather, wave at him over the bars. I found the ironing board and ironed my dress while Phoebe put on her makeup and Mom located enough of her outfit to be satisfied, even though the Robin Hood hat was temporarily AWOL. No one spoke until we were ready to go.

"Mom, I need to ask you a question," I said, as we headed toward the door. "Where are we exactly?"

She looked at me and sighed. "I don't really know, sweetheart," she said, taking my arm in hers. "But we're late. Let's go."

chapter eight

Dominoes

The religion we grew up with, besides Judaism, was sleeping late on Sundays. This was actually Mom's personal religion, which all her children adopted as their own. Dad was the one who would get up early and buy the papers and bagels, while the rest of us stayed tucked in until noon. And woe be unto whoever's friend made the mistake of calling before then, because that was worth a mood from Mom that could make the most unbearable day of the week even worse.

So when Frank told me, one Sunday morning at 10:15, that Phoebe had called, I was surprised. Since I've been married, my epic sleeps have disappeared because of the kids. The best I can do is usually 10:00, which, granted, is not bad, but it still feels like 5:00 A.M. to me. And they love making fun of my morning motif. "Coffee!" Simon booms, walking like a drunk to imitate me staggering toward the pot. (Not that he's too far off, I should add.) I make them breakfast and try to rouse myself in general, since Sunday is a day I can write without phone calls. Except for this particular Sunday, when I was hellbent on going to Saks to buy clothes, taking the direct approach for a change, instead of hoping I could find something in whichever catalogue appeared on my doorstep.

But Phoebe calling this early was odd. Maybe she's met a guy. Anything was possible, since I hadn't seen her much lately, except the night we spent at Mom's. She had worked on the independent feature film all summer and Frank and I had gone away on vacation during most of August. Then she was studying for her union exam, spending hours learning about different types of nails so she could be employed as a set dresser on a movie that actually paid a living wage.

Should I call her back now? I asked Frank. He nodded. "She said for you to call as soon as you got up."

I dialed. "What's wrong?"

"Did Frank tell you something was wrong?" Her tone seemed light, a little giddy.

"No, he just said to call. What's wrong?"

"Well, I don't want you to get mad, but I think I broke my foot."

"Why would I get mad? What happened?"

"Well, I went out drinking last night with some people and I went back to this guy's house, but I didn't stay there, it's all fucked up, it's a long story but he doesn't really want a relationship and I said fine, whatever, and so he walked me home and I fell."

"When was this?"

"About four-thirty this morning. And what happened was that I was wearing these lace-up shoes but I hadn't really laced them all the way because I had taken them off at his house. And we were crossing the street and I stepped off the curb and fell but I didn't hurt anything else. I just went down with all my weight on my foot."

I peeled strips of bacon out of the package. "Uh-huh. Then what happened?"

"Well, then I started to laugh, I was so embarrassed, and he asked if I was all right and I said I was fine but my foot really hurt like hell. So he walked me home and I didn't know what to do because if I called you that early and it wasn't broken you would kill me. And I couldn't call Mommy because she would freak that I was even out that late with a guy. So I called Stephen."

"At a quarter to five, you called Stephen?" (And he thought *I* was a difficult patient.) "What did he say?"

"That if it hurt the way I said it did I may have broken it and I should go to the emergency room and have it X-rayed." She started to cry.

"Phoebe, why didn't you call me when this happened?" I was getting upset now. She sounded scared.

"Because I didn't want to wake you up and find out there was nothing wrong and then you'd be mad at me."

"But this is an emergency! Do you want me to go to the hospital with you now? I will, but I have to make the kids breakfast first."

Now, why did I say that? Here she is on the other end of the phone, clearly terrified, not to mention being in pain.

"I can skip making the breakfast," I added quickly, sliding waffles into the toaster. "Do you want me to come with you now?"

"Well, I waited this long, so I don't think it matters," she said. "Could you be ready, like, in an hour?"

"Less than that. I just don't understand why you waited so long to call me." It was easier to work up anger at her than to stop and wonder why I was clinging to this idiotic notion of breakfast. Except to say that routine is the best reflex when you don't want to function. And boy, did I not want to, Why didn't she call Mommy? Why am I always the mommy?

I went into the living room where Frank and Simon were listening to music. Nat was still asleep. And he makes fun of *me*.

"Phoebe thinks she broke her foot," I said.

Frank nodded. "I know. She didn't want me to tell you."

"Why? What am I, a monster?"

Frank and Simon looked at each other and smiled. "Have some more coffee, honey."

With breakfast safely on the table I went around the corner to Phoebe's apartment, bringing my crutches, which I had saved, just in case. She showed me her foot; it was two, maybe three times the size it should be. And turning blue.

"Are you insane?" I shouted. "Look at this. It's a nightmare! Can't you see what it looks like?"

"I didn't want to know so I didn't look," she said.

Now that's logic.

We got a cab to the emergency room at Lenox Hill and she answered questions from a guy dressed in white who was not a doctor.

"What's your name?"

"Phoebe."

"Stevie?"

This was going to be a long day.

I followed her to the X-ray room. "I'm sitting right here, see me?" I said, outside the door. The technician came out and put the pictures on the light box, followed by Phoebe. "Yes, here it is. The bone is broken there and there."

"Shit!" She started to laugh. "I can't believe I did this."

A doctor appeared. Phoebe was sitting in a wheelchair now. "We need a urine sample," he said. "Take this in there." He pointed to a bathroom.

"Do you want me to help you?" I asked.

"Yes," she said. "Come with me."

We went into the bathroom, and, of course, she couldn't go. "Here, I'll run the water," I said, turning it on. "Listen, it's like a waterfall. *Whoosh, whoosh.*"

"Shut up," she said, laughing. "I can't do it. You've got to leave."

I waited for her outside the door, where, of course, there was no place to sit, except an extra wheelchair. I took it.

Finally, she came out.

"Listen, I think we'd better call Mommy," I said.

"No, way," Phoebe said emphatically. "She's going to kill me. How am I going to work now? Even if I got offered a movie I wouldn't be able to do it."

"Did you take your exam?" I asked.

"Oh, yeah, yesterday," she said. "I guess I did all right, I don't really know. I'm sure I'll fail like everyone else the first time."

The doctor reappeared. "So, what did you do?" he asked me. I looked up, horrified, and flew out of the wheelchair. "It's not me," I said. "It's her."

"Well, what did *you* do?" he shifted his gaze.

"I went out drinking and fell down drunk," she said, sweetly.

He nodded. "We're going to have to set the foot."

"Where's Stephen?" I blasted. "Are you an orthopedist?"

"No, but I can set it until she sees Stephen tomorrow. First, though"—he gestured to the form on his clipboard—"I need to know who to contact in an emergency."

"Barbara Witchel," Phoebe said promptly.

"Wait a minute," I said. "This *is* an emergency. Did you not call me? Am I not standing here with you?"

She started to laugh. "Sorry," she said and gave my address too.

"That's it, Phoebe. I'm calling Mommy. I can't believe you! I'm spending my whole day at the hospital and you're giving Mommy's name."

I called. No answer. "Don't leave a message," Phoebe said. "We'll do it later."

The doctor came into the room and made her lie on her stomach while he wrapped her foot with strips of plaster of Paris up to her knee and sort of molded it. She screamed into the pillow and I held her hand. When I had gone to Stephen for the shots in my ankle, I had stuck my head in her lap and screamed. Now I could return the favor.

On the way out she had to stop and fill out more forms. "Have you eaten, can I get you something?" I asked. She shook her head no.

"You should have something," I insisted. It's our heritage. When in crisis, eat. I went down the street to the Butterfield Market, which has great sandwiches, but they were closed. I came back with a Milky Way from the corner newsstand.

She looked at it with utter disdain. "I don't want that," she said.

"Okay. I'll eat it." I was suddenly aware that I was about to faint. I'd been so busy making everyone else breakfast that I hadn't had any and I could not get the picture of that big, blue foot out of my mind.

We went outside and I hailed a cab. "You get in first," she said. So I did. "We're going to the West Side," I said to the driver, who immediately hit the accelerator.

"Wait!" Phoebe and I both yelled. She had gotten herself in but not the crutches. "Don't you even wait for the door to close?" I yelled again. What an asshole. For the rest of the ride he scowled at me in the rearview mirror while I craned my neck, giving meaningful and menacing glances at his identification on the dashboard.

Finally, we were back in Phoebe's apartment. It was 1:30.

"Okay," she said, resigned. "You can call Mommy. I can't."

I picked up the phone. "Hi, Mom, I tried you before, where were you?"

"Dad and I took a walk, it's so beautiful out today." She was in her tranquil, communing-with-nature mode.

"Mom, I'm calling from Phoebe's apartment." In the abrupt silence on the other end, I could hear her antennae go up. "We just came back from Lenox Hospital. She broke her foot."

"*What?*"

Phoebe covered her face with a pillow. "I told you," she mumbled.

"She was walking home last night and she fell off the curb," I went on. "I think you should come in."

"When did this happen?"

"About four-thirty," I said.

"In the *morning?* What was she doing out at four-thirty in the morning?"

"Uh, this guy was walking her home."

"This *guy?*"

"I told you," Phoebe moaned from underneath the pillow.

"Listen, just come in, will you?" I said. "I have to go to Saks and I've been with her for hours. She needs to have this prescription for painkillers filled and she's not on my medical plan."

I was getting mad at Mom now, even though I shouldn't have. If this had happened to me, I would have called her no matter what time it was. And I know she would have come, just as she would have for Phoebe. So it wasn't as if she was avoiding this and making me do it. Phoebe was avoiding this and making me do it.

The whole thing was like dominoes, really. Mommy grew up learning never to ask for anything because even though she had polio she wanted to prove that she was just as good as everyone else if not better—always better—so I grew up the same way. Only, small detail, I never had polio. And instead of my being free to resent that, as any self-respecting daughter should, Phoebe grows up with Mommy *and* me as double examples of women who never ask for anything. So not only is it Mommy's fault that Phoebe was lying in bed with a broken foot for six hours and doing nothing about it, but suddenly it's also mine and I don't even have children. How did that happen?

"We'll be there very soon," Mom said, switching to her capable mode, and hung up.

"All right, Mommy's coming, your emergency next of kin."

I heard myself. I'm mad at being considered a mother and then I'm mad when I'm not. I'm so focused on how wrong it is that Phoebe can't ask for anything that I don't notice how convinced I am that if I don't push the button on the toaster myself, no one in my house can eat breakfast. Or will ever love me again, because I should automatically be able to stand in the emergency room of Lenox Hill Hospital and cook in my kitchen at the same time.

I remember when I was flying up from Brownies to Girl Scouts. This was quite an event in my life, needless to say, and my troop had planned the ceremony for weeks. All the mothers were coming, even mine, even though it was on a school day. So, there we all were waiting for the mothers to arrive and all of them did. Except mine. We waited some more until finally we had to start. And just as we did, the door opened and in swept Mom, breathless, with a big smile on her face, eager to be the proud mother of a brand-new Girl Scout. And at that particular moment I saw Robin Cohen's mother turn to Barbara Packer's mother and make an absolutely dreadful face that said quite clearly, "Oh, so the professorial princess has deigned to join us."

And instead of being mad at Mom for being late I was suddenly furious with both these women who had the nerve to make any face at all about my mother, who was having it all and doing it all twenty-five years before most women even began to realize that it couldn't be done. When I flew up, she was sitting in her chair beaming and everything was as it should be.

Or not. I'm exhausted now just thinking about it, how she pushed herself so mercilessly. And how easily I followed suit. Strive for perfection in all things and achieve perfection in all things. No excuses. No "but I did the best I can." If the best you could wasn't good enough, then by definition it wasn't the best. God. And all this from Grandma picking the wrong day and the wrong municipal pool to go swimming in sixty years ago, which has set off a generational echo chamber for each one that follows: not worth it, not worth it, not worth it.

And here I was now, desperately trying to separate from Mom, trying to become myself whether she liked it or not. Whether I liked it or not. And we were tied in how much neither one of us liked it at all.

I think I became consciously aware of my struggle when I was in the middle of the ankle trauma. With me wearing a cast and walking with crutches, Frank and I went on vacation. We couldn't go to Venice, which is where he really wanted to take me. (I'd never been to Italy, even though Phoebe spent her junior year in college there. Talk about bills!) So, we went to northern California instead and spent our first night in San Francisco. Near the hotel was a Walgreens or one of those pharmacies that stay open all night and one of us needed something and in we went. Frank disappeared down an aisle and as I walked around the front, an older man approached me.

"Barbara?" he asked. My mother's name. He was calling me by my mother's name.

I looked at him. He had gray hair and a black beret and what Mom would call a crazy look in his eye.

"No," I said, trying to crutch away.

But he moved in front of me. "Is it polio?" he asked, his tone solicitous.

I thought my heart would stop.

"What?"

"Is it? Is that why you're using the crutches?" he asked.

I felt myself get cold. Did he actually just say this to me? Who was this man? Could he possibly have known Mommy when she was younger? But why was he using the present tense? Didn't he know that time had passed? That I had stood in line for hours in the vast gymnasium of a public school with Mom right behind me to drink a caramel-flavored liquid from a paper cup so I would never get polio? And that was at least thirty years ago. Didn't he know that I had never been allowed to swim in a municipal pool in my entire life?

Or maybe time had reversed, somehow, like in *The Twilight Zone*. Where was I? Who was I? I kept looking at his face, trying to speak.

"It was in Maine," he continued. "Is that where you're from?"

"No," I finally answered. "No, I'm not."

And then the cashier called "Next" and he started to walk away, seeming to forget about me as quickly as he had found me.

I moved down an aisle, away from him. I didn't know what to do. Just which one of us was crazy, anyway? I took three pairs of stockings off the shelf, which was a total waste of time and money since I couldn't wear them with a cast on. I just wanted my leg back. And I wanted to be me, suddenly more than ever. Right now.

I found Frank, and told him what happened. As we left, I checked up and down the block to make sure the man was gone.

He was. And Frank didn't know what to make of it any more than I did.

I called Mom. "Did you ever spend time in Maine when you were growing up?" I asked. "When you were on crutches or in a cast or after an operation?"

"No," she said. She had only visited Maine with Dad, as an adult.

I told her why I wanted to know. "My God, what do you think it means?" I asked, still shaken.

"It means this man knew someone in Maine named Barbara who had polio, that's all," she said flatly. "Why does it have to mean anything? Where do you get these strange ideas?"

I didn't know. But I knew this definitely meant something. It had to.

"Where are those shoes you were wearing, by the way?" I asked Phoebe.

She pointed toward the kitchen. André Assous canvas platform espadrilles with long strings that tie up the leg. I noticed that the canvas on the left one was completely ripped from the platform.

"Uh, Phoebe, can I ask you a question?"

"Mmmmm," she said, feeling the painkillers they gave her at the hospital, which didn't quite cover the prospect of having to face my parents with six months of medical bills and no job.

"Did you break your right foot?"

"Uh-huh."

"Then could you explain to me why your left shoe is ripped?"

She sat up, staring.

"Phoebe, you put your shoes on the wrong feet. That's why you tripped, not because it wasn't tied up all the way. It was on the wrong foot!"

"Oh, my God!" She started to laugh.

"You fucking spaz!" I laughed too. "Why did you take the damn things off in the first place?"

"I don't know! Oh, my God! I can't tell Daddy. He'll kill me."

"Yeah, and Mommy won't? I'm leaving. This is not a scene I want to witness."

"*No!* You can't go. Please? You have to stay until they come. You're my protection."

"Aaaagh." What else is new? I looked out the window. "Okay," I said, "but after they come I'm going to Saks."

"Okay," she agreed. I looked around. "I'll make you some tea. Where's the bed tray I got you?" Earlier in the summer, when she was working twenty-hour days and sleeping on the movie set, I found a catalogue selling rattan bed trays with side slots for magazines and they looked so decadent (and were on sale) that I bought one for me and one for Phoebe, with the idea that when it was all over she could lie here and languish.

She squirmed. Then she looked as if she was going to say something, but having already spent the day caught in the headlights, sur-rendered quickly.

"I gave it to my friend Carla," she said. "I wasn't going to use it. I have no room for it."

"Oh. Okay." I tried to seem fine about this. But this is why I don't like giving gifts. Did she think I was implying she was lazy? Was this gift her version of *Between Parent and Child*? Did she resent it? I thought she'd like it.

An hour later the car pulled up. Finally. "Where have you been?" I asked Mom, who came in carrying groceries.

"I stopped at the cash machine and bought a few things and there was traffic."

Among the "few things" was a ten-pound bag of sugar. "Well, thank God you brought this, so she can start turning out some cakes and pies tonight," I said. "Mom, she's on crutches. She can't put any weight on her foot!"

"Be quiet," she said, going to Phoebe. "Show me." She looked at the temporary cast and at the X-rays. "Yes, I see the breaks," she said, immediately, pointing them out.

I held up the shoe. "What's wrong with this picture?" I asked Mom. She looked blank. "Left shoe ripped, right foot broken. Get it?"

"Oh, Phoebe," Mom breathed. "Honestly."

The bell rang. It was Dad.

"Okay, girls," I said, "I'm making a quick exit now."

"No!" Phoebe looked panicked. "Just a little longer."

I stayed. No fireworks. Dad was pretty laid back about it, actu-ally. Then he left to take her prescription to the pharmacy. So far so good.

"'Bye, I'll call you later." I got my bag.

"Alex, thank you so much." She looked small and woebegone in the bed. And pale.

I practically ran into the street. This was going to be my day when I was going to do something for me and what happens? For the nine thousandth time I am taking care of my family. Or more specifically, I am taking care of the kids.

I got in a cab, to save time, I decided, while trying not to notice that my ankle had started to hurt, in sympathy, no doubt. I thought about feet. There was a definite problem in this family with the women being able to stand on them. First there was Grandma, who was born with flat feet and was still talking about them seventy years later. She used to tell me long, elaborately detailed stories about the pain she felt when she was growing up, and how she was given iron arches to put inside her shoes. She would describe her foot slamming against the iron wedges on her way up and down the stairs of her family's sixth-floor walk-up apartment.

Then, of course, there was Mom and her foot. And me with mine. Now Phoebe. What the hell was going on?

I got out at Saks and headed with great purpose up the escalators, tearing through racks of clothes, gathering armloads of outfits, zipping and unzipping, buttoning and unbuttoning. I was a living tornado, sweeping up anything and everything in my path. Twenty-four try-ons later, I had one dress. One.

I pushed my sweatpants off the dressing-room chair and sat down. It was only four o'clock. I felt a hundred years old. And I felt like a shit.

What kind of situation is it when my own sister doesn't want to call me to help her? And when she does, all I can do is tell her I have to go shopping? Have I gotten so selfish I can't do anything for anyone else? Or am I just so angry I won't?

I have no reason to be angry with Phoebe. She is always there for me, loyal and available. Yet every time I plan an activity, I manage to exclude her from at least part of it. Why? To prove how powerful

I am? How powerful can I be if I need to do that? Yes, she knows I love her and have always taken care of her, but my actions now can't possibly inspire great confidence in my commitment to her. Maybe I wouldn't have called me either.

I looked in the mirror. My hair was dirty, there were purple circles under my eyes and I thought I could already see that Milky Way on my chin. My legs looked fat, my arms looked fat, my back hurt. A prize, through and through.

So, she wouldn't ask for help when she needed it. Should that shock me? Do I? Does Mom? Hah. When my ankle started to swell and Stephen told me to stop working out, stop cooking, stop running around, I laughed in his face. Ask someone to do something *for* me? Unthinkable.

I looked down at my big, wide feet and thought about Chinese women with their tiny bound feet, who weren't allowed to even try standing on them or standing up for themselves. And I realized that in my family, though we may like to think of ourselves as pioneers, leaders of women and forces of nature, we are bound. We do not stand up and say no. We fight to be superlative at all costs. We stand tall on our bound feet until we fall over with exhaustion from the terrible effort to achieve while asking for nothing. We are women. This is what we do. We shouldn't. We should say no, like men. But we don't.

I do as my mother does. Which horrifies her no end. "Do you think I *wanted* polio?" she asked me as if I were demented, when I was explaining the theory of my ankle problems to her. Well, no, Mom. I knew you didn't want it. I also knew that, logic aside, I would do anything to be just like her. Growing up and grown up, mothers are there for a reason, for comfort, for guidance, for the guarantee from God that you are not alone, never alone, because there's someone else alive who you were once a physical part of. (And don't you forget it.)

But the way we play the woman game, who can win? The answer is no one, not even Mom. Grandma used to tell me the story about her oldest brother, Max, sending her downstairs to buy him chocolate. Being a girl and the fifth child of six left her in an unlucky position. There she'd go, with her iron arches, banging down six flights of stairs and back again while Max sat with a stopwatch and timed her. Timed her! Did she ever say, "Fuck you, Max, you sadistic son of a bitch. Do you realize when we grow up each one of us is going to get midlife onset diabetes because we're *all* eating too much sugar?" No. She ran like hell. He got his chocolate. And she made great time, doing his bidding.

Just as she taught my mother to do my father's. And her children's. And last and most certainly least, her own. So that's what I learned too, with that big "not worth it" ringing in my ears. Big surprise, then, that Phoebe didn't call me. To her, I set the same standard of perfection as Mom, our Statue of Liberty, the great lady with book and light, bigger than life, inspiring you, daring you, threatening you to be free. There's an arm that never gets tired. We should all be made of copper.

But if Phoebe sees me floating above her, lost in the perfection zone, that is not where I find myself. I am the middle of the perfection sandwich. For me to make Mom happy I need to be more, more, more, always. For me to make Phoebe happy I need to be less, less, less, so there's only one Supreme Being for her to worry about. Most of the time, though, there is no sandwich, only hash. Mom is me and I am her and Phoebe is both of us, even though she's most like Grandma, which then echoes double for Mom. In the end not one of us can stand up, because she has too many other people sitting on top of her, and so the feet, the ankles, the legs give right out. Phoebe should have kept that bed tray and I should have gotten one for Mom too. We should all have had them surgically attached.

I paid for the dress and found the phones.

"How are you?" I asked.

"Fine." She sounded sleepy. "It's starting to hurt now. Mommy and I are taking a nap. Daddy's doing my laundry."

He's doing her laundry? Good Lord. He's not going to kill her after all. Ever since that bedroom wall, this girl can do anything.

"That's good," I said. "I'm going home to take a shower and get dressed for dinner, but I'll stop by and see you later."

Which I did.

She looked better. Mom had straightened up the apartment and Dad was watching television. "Thank you, sweetheart," Mom said, taking me aside. "I really appreciate what you did today and I feel better knowing that you're right around the corner because I can't be."

"That's okay, Mom. I know."

Later, I lay in bed, first getting to the Sunday papers. The phone rang. I looked at the clock. 12:40 A.M.

"Alex, my foot is turning purple."

"What?"

"It really is, the toes at the end of the cast are purple. That doctor wrapped these Ace bandages too tight around the splint. I've got to take them off."

"But, Phoebe, he said to keep the splint on so it would be immobilized."

She started to cry. "I know you think I'm crazy, but I'm not. Something is wrong here."

"Okay, I believe you. Do you want to go to the emergency room?"

"Yes."

"Fine, but you know what? First you should call Stephen and find out what he says because if it's that painful, maybe you shouldn't be swinging it in and out of cabs."

"But it hurts."

"I know, Phoebe, but call him first. And if he thinks you should go, I'll come over and take you. Okay?"

I was trying to be good here. She was actually asking for something. But I distinctly heard that doctor say not to move it around.

A few minutes later the phone rang again. She was much calmer.

"Stephen told me to loosen the Ace bandages which I did and it feels better. Tomorrow I'll see him and get a real cast."

"Well that's great. Sleep well and I'll speak to you tomorrow. I'm really glad you called me."

I was.

I brought her lunch the next day, the day after that and the day after that. "Guess what?" she said. "I passed my union exam."

"Oh, Phoebe, that's fabulous! I can't believe you did it the first time!"

"I know, I thought I failed."

"Now, why would you think that? You're so much smarter than you ever give yourself credit for."

"Well, I can't work now, anyway," she said. "Stephen said not for at least three months. And I also have to be voted on and ratified by a certain number of union members, so it's not like I'm actually in yet."

"So what? The hardest part is over. You made it. Be a little proud of yourself."

Finally, she smiled. "I know. I really can't believe it."

Later that night I came back. I folded some laundry and unloaded the dishwasher.

"Can you stay awhile?" she asked. Her face looked pinched. And lonely.

"Well, I really have more work to do tonight."

As soon as the words were out of my mouth, I felt ashamed. Why could I not just give her what she asked for? Without negotiation? Or making her feel that she's a second choice? And, besides, why shouldn't I stay and (God forbid!) relax a little? For a change. I had worked the entire day and it was already 10:00 P.M. Was I going to keep running myself eternally into the ground in the hopes that, tomorrow maybe, I'd wake up perfect? Look, Mom! Solid copper, through and through!

"You know what?" I said. "Forget work. I'm happy to stay."

"Oh, great!" She glowed with relief.

I lay down next to her and she flipped the remote. Mary Tyler Moore was on, she said. That sounded good. I put my feet up on the pillows, next to her cast, and tickled her big toe with mine. She laughed.

Mary threw her hat in the air. And why the hell not?

chapter nine

Queen of the Possums

I must say that I have always found Mom's secret ambition to be a
nun more than a little odd.

That's right, a nun. The idea seemed to fascinate her. I can
only guess that with four screaming children and a full-time job, the
notion of devoting herself to an utterly silent being was irresistible.
Actually, one of her closest friends was a nun, Sister Jeanette, whom
she had met at Iona College when she started teaching there in 1970.

Sister Jeanette was something of a radical (of course, Mom im-
printed on a radical nun, as any upstanding Jewish girl would) because she was an outspoken opponent of wearing habits at a time when
church officials were insisting they be required. Mom would visit Sister
Jeanette where she lived with her order, in the Bronx, I think, and bring
them big chocolate cakes from the Scarsdale Pastry Center to liven up
their dinners.

Then Sister Jeanette started taking Mom with her on retreat, to a

place called The Queen of Apostles, somewhere out in the country, so
Mom could spend a weekend in a narrow room with a cot and ponder
her life. I started calling her Queen of the Possums. "Fresh child," she
would reply, shaking her head.

But when Sister Jeanette eventually took on missionary duty in El
Salvador, Mom stayed home. I guess they didn't have possums in El
Salvador.

I always figured that part of this nun fantasy was Mom's passive
aggression about certain distasteful aspects of Orthodox Jewry, like the
tyranny of the kosher kitchen and sitting behind bars at temple. But in
a larger sense, I think it meant freedom from the drudgery of the ev-
eryday world, a place where she wouldn't have to make piles. In Mom's
nun wish, earthly affairs would never be allowed to interfere with affairs of the spirit. (Wouldn't the logical extension also be no affairs of
the flesh?) I couldn't help but notice that being a nun also meant that.

Like most mothers when it came to sex, mine was the supreme
keeper of the double message. Sex was good. Sex was fun. Sex was
important (because of procreation, which we would certainly hate to
forget). But the key element of the message was that, somehow, sex
is all these things for mothers and none of these things for daughters.
Until they grew up and got married.

When that happened then, yes, by all means, Phoebe and I both
should instantly become wildly passionate sexual beings. With no practice. There we would be on our wedding nights (in diaphanous pei-
gnoirs trimmed with lace and satin ribbons) looking virginal and lovely
and voilà! Rev up like Sharon Stone in *Basic Instinct*.

Actually, all pretense of propriety aside, Mom now claims she really did know what was going on behind the den doors with me and
Ricky Plotkin while she sat in the kitchen, and maybe she did. It was
what went on behind those doors when he slept over (being my camp
boyfriend from Queens qualified him for overnight privileges as a for-

eign visitor) when I got up at three in the morning and went downstairs to visit him that she hadn't quite counted on.

It wasn't that she wouldn't discuss sex. You might just say that in our house "don't ask, don't tell" was an effective policy long before the rest of the country caught on. She would discuss it if she absolutely had to, but usually from the rather clinical perspective of women's health. Mom was big on both *Our Bodies, Ourselves* and Planned Parenthood—but only eventually. When I was sixteen and had cystitis, she took me to the pediatrician and seemed to actually believe me when I told her I got it from sitting around in a wet bathing suit. In October.

Okay. Maybe she knew more than she let on. God knows she's always advocated privacy. And with Grandma for a mother that was probably the best policy, since Grandma had unyielding notions of both propriety and biology. This was a woman who, in kindergarten at a New York City public school, refused, at the age of five, to play ring-around-the-rosy with the rest of the class because she thought the girl standing next to her had filthy hands and she didn't want to hold them.

And if that's how she felt about girls, when it came to boys, don't ask. With the exception of Izzy Twersky who seemingly could do no wrong, they all fell into the category of "only wanting one thing," a philosophy that apparently made quite an impression on Mom, since both Phoebe and I heard it too.

When it came to body awareness no one beat Grandma. When she was pregnant with her youngest son, who was born ten years after Mom's other brother, she thought it was menopause. This from a woman who already had two children and didn't even recognize she was about to have a third. That sort of mindset put a definite damper on a free and easy environment in which to discuss sexuality. Or to even acknowledge it. Though the pictures and home movies of Mom as a teenager were pretty hot, à la Rita Hayworth. She had long black hair and a bright red mouth and seemed to always be wearing something off the shoulder. And she was a real dating expert, to hear her tell it, sometimes juggling two or three guys in a night. One before dinner, one during, one after. But by the time I was in junior high school, asking questions, they had all turned into study dates. Subject unknown.

Mom never pressured me about the details of sex, but she encouraged basic knowledge about the equipment, like being sure I was properly fitted for a diaphragm. Too bad she couldn't control the intangibles, like my complete lack of coordination. I'm sure I wasn't the only female in American who despaired of ever getting a grasp on that slippery thing as it went shooting through my fingers yet again. It really did prove a much more effective method of birth control than even the Pill, because by the time you were done chasing it around the guy was fast asleep.

Once I was married, Mom and I didn't discuss sex anymore. Now it was really private; the fact that Frank was a husband placed him above evaluation or reproach. Never mind that on our first date when he asked me up to his apartment "for a cup of tea," a cup I might add I'm still waiting for, we talked until 4:00 A.M. despite his best efforts to get me into bed. Not that I wouldn't have done it, mind you, but five days before I met him I had gone off the Pill in a fit of pique, convinced I'd never meet a man worth sleeping with again.

Then there was the whole condom issue, which people much younger than I seemed to deal with better. I mean, Frank was divorced and, appearances to the contrary, he was clearly not sitting home alone at night drinking tea. And there I was coming out of a long-term relationship, having had no opportunity to perfect my condom technique (when last I checked, the boy usually carried an ancient one in his wallet for display purposes, but times had most definitely changed). Frank had the more up-to-date approach. Somehow his conversation managed to include a reference early on to a recent physical where "everything was fine."

Health concerns aside, I knew he was a child of the sixties, who seemed to have spent the better part of his years at Harvard getting stoned and getting laid and not necessarily in that order. I had spent the better part of my years at Wheaton learning to balance a teacup on my knee without spilling a drop on my escort's topsiders.

Phoebe, of course, has to deal with all the health worries much more than I ever did. When she met someone recently whom she liked (and who was more together than the other guy, the one she was with on the night she broke her foot), he asked, on their way home, "Do we have to stop at the drugstore?" Just like that. And she said yes and so they did.

But apart from stuff like that, sex is not something she and I talk about terribly much, which is weird because we talk about everything else. I mentioned that to her once. "No one in our family talks about sex," she said, matter-of-factly. "When you're old enough, Mommy gives you a copy of *Our Bodies, Ourselves* and wishes you luck."

Since she had broken her foot, Phoebe had gotten another hostessing job to tide her through her healing period. She was offered other movies, but she couldn't take them. So this time, she was working at the JUdson Grill, near the theater district. And soon discovered she had a new friend. Some creepy guy who apparently spent his days calling restaurants where the phones are mostly answered by women, asking their names and then asking about the state of their underwear. But he hadn't counted on Phoebe.

"I told him my name when he asked," she told me later. "Then he asked if I was wearing any underwear. And I said, 'Yeah.' He said, 'What kind?' And I said, 'Well I think they're white, actually, with black flowers.'" Her tone was completely businesslike. I started to laugh.

"What did he say then?"

"Well, then he asked if I was wearing a bra, but the other phones were ringing so I said, 'Yes,' and he said, 'What color?' and I said, 'I'll get right back to you,' and put him on hold to answer the other phones. But he hung up."

I found this hilarious. Especially when he called back a month or two later. "Who's this?" he asked.

"Phoebe," she said.

"Are you wearing underwear?" he asked.

"Oh, are we doing this again?" she said. "Yes. White and white. Anything else?"

Apparently not. He hung up.

Mom and I actually did discuss sex once after I was married. It all started with the new nightgown she bought me after our stay at the Stanhope, when she became thoroughly disgusted with the state of my lingerie. It was Christian Dior, cream-colored and trimmed with lace.

I knew it was trouble the minute I saw it. It's like owning good gloves. Or scarves. I know myself well enough not to. I have never owned a pair of leather gloves lined in silk as Mom does. I buy wool knit gloves on the street for five dollars, or from the J.Crew sale catalogue in July. And last year when I finally dropped eighty bucks on a cashmere scarf, I left it at a luncheon, found it, then lost it again on the street one rainy night when I was achieving the incredibly complex feat of putting on my coat while simultaneously hailing a cab.

Anyway, the nightgown. Sure enough, within the first month of ownership, I took it on a business trip to Los Angeles with Frank and left it there. No problem. The hotel mailed it back. Months went by. But the more it was laundered the weirder it got. Maybe it was the dryer that did it, but the material got sort of sticky. The hem rolled up. As per usual, I paid no attention. If it was clean, I wore it. One night I got into bed, where I found Frank, eager to remove it. Happy to oblige, I started to pull it off with him. Blue and purple sparks flew into the air.

"What was that?" he asked. It was clearly too soon for me to take credit for flashing lights, so I didn't even try.

"My nightgown is short-circuiting," I said, pulling it off to crackling lightning. "The one my mother bought me. It's a chastity nightgown. You may think you have conjugal rights, but Mom knows better."

Well, Mom thought this was just the funniest thing she had ever heard, though I neglected to tell her the end of the story. That the next morning, I threw it out. Before Frank did.

But she had more important things on her mind during that particular time than monitoring my inventory of appropriate lingerie. Like her longstanding Captain Kirk fantasy. Yes, God help me, James Tiberius Kirk, captain of the starship U.S.S. *Enterprise*, appearing on screens nationwide in *Star Trek: Generations* for what threatened to be the last time, because in this installment he died. But, as we all know, the great thing about movies and the even greater thing about science fiction is that death means never having to miss a sequel. Which came as small comfort to Mom. This time he was (supposedly) really gone.

Naturally, Mom having crushes on fictional characters or movie stars fell into the category of acceptable lust. (Though if she was going to pursue the nun thing, she'd have to learn to lust a little more quietly.) For all the talk, or lack thereof, about sex that she had with me or Phoebe, it was practically nonexistent when the tables turned. Which was fine, I guess. I certainly didn't expect her to wax poetic about sex with Dad. And there were oblique references to a few good kissers among all those dates. But who were her Ricky Plotkins? I was somewhat curious, but not overly so, if the truth be told. A mother's sex life has definite parameters. As her child, I just expected her to know about it without necessarily doing it. As my mother, she expected the same from me. But this Captain Kirk thing had been going on since I was nine or ten, now that I focused on it. She certainly was loyal.

I, of course, could not be less interested in Captain Kirk, or for that matter William Shatner. I watched *Star Trek* under duress as a child and today was no different. But here was the moment she'd waited for. I was interviewing him for the *Times* and she was coming with me, fresh from a screening. That was if she could make it in her distraught state, having just watched the object of her affection croak. Her mascara blotted for the umpteenth time, we walked into Orso, and there he was, alive, wearing a suit, and still in orange pancake makeup from a slew of television appearances touting his cinematic death.

"Mom, calm down. We're having lunch with him," I had reminded her on the way over. "He's not *really* dead."

"We're having lunch with William Shatner," she sniffed. "It's not quite the same."

Well, as *Star Trek* fans go, she deserved ten bonus points for knowing the difference. But did he? Could he? Was it possible for someone to be the triumphant leader of good over evil in every galaxy for three decades and still call his agent in the morning?

We seated ourselves, with him in the middle. He was a youngish-looking sixty-three, wearing a dark brown jacket, light brown shirt, brown print tie and brown paisley handkerchief in his jacket pocket. Between this and his face he looked like sunset in the Sahara.

Mom leapt right in. How forward!

"Are you sad it's over?" she asked earnestly.

"Yes and no," he began. "It's like a marriage and a divorce. You get divorced and you're very sad but there is a feeling that time moves on, things change and maybe it's fate decreeing change is in the air." He gave a sly smile. "All those clichés." Which made me wonder why he was using them. But Mom didn't flinch.

"I had to play the character so closely to me," he went on, "that when it came time to perform a death scene I had to think what it would be like to die." He looked deep into her eyes, Kirk, ladykiller to the core. "I don't know how you feel about it, but I'm having too much fun for that. Are you?"

"I'm more realistic," she declared. Good old literal Mom. Neither lust, romance or good old-fashioned star-fucking could get in her way. His brown back went up.

"I'm saying *emotionally* I don't want to go," he huffed, "so I had to imagine going through the part of the mind that shuts off about this. I had to think about my last breath."

Now, if our positions were switched and he was my fantasy figure, I would develop a quick and lethal case of food poisoning from whatever it was I had eaten for breakfast, and disappear, pronto. But Mom was in for the long haul. She had invested years, nay, decades in this man's heroism, leaping whole solar systems in a single bound, and a little-less-than-sparkling lunch conversation was not making a dent. There really is no accounting for taste.

Kirk's death scene had prompted a dissection of the exact meaning of his last words, "Oh my."

"You tell me what you thought it meant first," he instructed Mom.

"That as he dies, it's what he sees beyond," she offered.

"Bless you," he said, beaming a benediction. "As an actor, I had to look at the threshold and beyond and see how scary that is. We all wear the rose-colored glasses of life. All of us, every human being, rejects death as the indisputable future which may be an instant away." He spoke only to Mom, who listened, heart and soul. I tried to imagine what color orange becomes when seen through the rose-colored glasses of life.

"Trying to die as Captain Kirk," he went on, "I hoped to convey that the whole time had been fun. I think the character would see death and greet it with the same mixture of awe and humor he always had."

Mom's eyes filled with tears yet again, reliving the moment of Kirk's death. Shatner was pleased. "I make you cry and I cry again myself," he said. "You can see why I loved the character and so you followed me through to the moment of my dying. I'm really deeply complimented." He reached out to hold her arm and mine. I don't know why he bothered with me. I had no idea what either one of them was talking about and I had just seen the movie.

Undaunted, he continued gazing at me à la Kirk. You could almost hear a sound track, any sound track, swell in the background. His left eye was thoroughly bloodshot.

"How come your eye is red?" I asked in my best journalistic manner.

"Oh, it's my contact," he said, flustered. "One is for reading and one is for distance."

"That's what I have," Mom said, her tone shifting to Dr. Mom. "It's time to take it out."

"God, I wish she was my mother," he said. "Can you lend her to me for a weekend?" He grinned. She grinned back. Thank God the food came.

Then Mom got confessional. "When *Apollo 13* was on its way to the moon and it got into trouble, I thought, 'Where is Captain Kirk?' And then I thought, 'Barbara, how could you?'" He studied her. "But it had such an effect on me," she continued, "you sitting on the bridge, the person in charge who always made the right decision."

He was transfixed. The earth had moved suitably for him to finally ask about her. The ultimate sacrifice. When she told him she was a college professor and administrator his condescension evaporated.

"You know, I think people with lesser knowledge of the world may cling to something like *Star Trek*, but for someone as educated, sophisticated and profound as yourself, it appeals to your intellect and something deeper within you."

Profound? Did someone say profound?

"I have another memory of you," Mom went on. "In *Twilight Zone*."

"Which one?" he asked, leaning in, fascinated. I remembered

Mom's advice, lo, those many years ago, about how to talk to boys. Talk about *them*, she had counseled. Well, she wasn't kidding. No wonder she had three dates a night.

Then he signed her copy of his book, the soul of graciousness. His publicist reappeared, signaling that it was time to go back to his hotel. "So soon?" he said in her direction, then turned back to us. "Do you want to come?" he asked, as if the notion of being separated from two such delicate flowers of nature was simply more than he could bear. Mom looked a little taken aback. Life was certainly less complicated in the black chair, wielding the remote control. Not only did she not have to put out, or even consider it under the vastly disapproving eye of her firstborn, but she could make him disappear, all with one button. He looked at me and I laughed pleasantly along the lines of ho, ho, ho, you should live so long.

He stood and shook my hand. Mom stayed seated. He leaned over and—did I believe my eyes?—kissed her on the mouth. With her head tilted back her neck looked soft and young. Then he cupped the side of her face in his hand and kissed her again. Her eyes were closed. And then once more, before exiting stage right. I was completely and utterly horrified. This was my *mother* after all. The woman who gave bottles, changed diapers and sewed name tapes into socks for camp. The same woman who had undoubtedly had sex only four times in her life for the sole purpose of creating each of us.

We watched him go.

"Am I blushing?" she asked.

"Actually, your face is maroon."

She lit a cigarette and opened the book. "Let me see what he said." She read, "To Barbara: I hope I haven't disappointed you. Bill."

Not likely. She was radiant.

"So, Earth to Mom. What did you think? Could you tell the difference between him and the character?"

"Yes," she said gravely, studying the tablecloth. "I felt I was having lunch with William Shatner." She lifted her chin. "I was kissed, however, by Captain Kirk."

Well, okay. It felt mean to point out that he seemed a tad less than ideal. She had had this fantasy about him for so long, it seemed a shame to lose it now. It was like anonymous sex. The person can be whoever you want and then disappear and be whoever they really are when you're not looking. Not that I would know that from personal experience, of course. Being the daughter of an aspiring nun, it would be unseemly to even think of such a thing.

A few cigarettes later, Mom's afterglow had subsided enough for us both to go back to work. I called Phoebe. "You would not believe what happened," I told her. "Captain Kirk kissed Mommy on the mouth."

"*What?*"

"Three times."

"*What?*"

"I'm not kidding."

"Well, what did she do?"

"She kissed him back."

"She did? Yuck."

"Tell me about it. I couldn't believe it. And he was holding her face like it was a movie."

"Is she going to tell Daddy?"

"Well, if she doesn't, he and a few million other people are going to read about it in the *Times,* anyway."

"You're going to *write* about it?"

"Well, how can I not? She's waited her entire life to meet him, she was totally swept away and he was loving every minute of it. Though I must say it was more than a little disgusting to sit there and watch my own mother suck face with Captain Kirk."

"With *tongues?* They kissed with *tongues?*"

"No, Phoebe, no tongues. Please. I just ate."

Later I called Mom.

"So, how's the little sex kitten?" I asked.

"What?"

So much for afterglow.

"How're you doing, Ma? Back among the living? Or still surfing Saturn's rings?"

The latter, apparently. We talked for a while, and her voice sounded downright dreamy. And she thanked me. For about the hundredth time.

When I hung up the phone, I realized that what I should have done when he suggested going to his hotel was to artfully disappear while somehow making sure Mom went—with the chastity nightgown! It certainly would have redefined the term *Starship Enterprise.* And as the good Lord only knows, it would have come in handy for a girl trying to keep her vows.

chapter ten

Divine Haven

I'm not sure when we decided to go, but Mom and I got into this big discussion about how she had never actually seen the Statue of Liberty on her fourth-grade field trip, because when they got there, it was closed. Brilliantly planned.

She had never been back, though she said that the memory of the bologna sandwich on white bread with mustard she had eaten on the ferry had stayed with her ever since. And as we talked about it, the rumblings began ever so slightly off in the distance, circling closer, ever closer. What could it be? A bird? A plane? No! It was Alex to the rescue, (still!) the best child on the face of the earth ensuring that if Mom still wanted to see the Statue of Liberty in all its tarnished glory, then her childhood wish was my adult command. After all, she's lived right here in New York for the fifty-four years since that trip was attempted. What possible opportunity could she have had to rectify the situation without *me?*

Which was how we ended up on the 9:45 A.M. ferry one Friday morning, Mom all smiles, Phoebe all glares. She knew that as far as credit was concerned this one was mine. She peered at the statue in the distance. "Look, it's pretty. Let's go to lunch."

Mom ignored her, firmly ensconced in her own rhapsody. "What a beautiful face," she murmured, clutching her plastic bag close. It actually did not contain a bologna sandwich on white bread, just a plain bagel and two oranges. Peeled. Just in case anyone planned on dying of malnutrition between breakfast and the elaborate lunch we were having at the Gotham Bar and Grill, one of New York's best restaurants. The promise of which, I might add, was the only way I could get Phoebe to come at all. But that would be later. Right now, as the boat *putt-putted* past Ellis Island, we were indulging an immigrant fantasy. Even though Mom's parents were both born here.

"Let's talk in an accent and pretend we're not from New York," Phoebe suggested. "Add some fun to this day."

Her specific problem was that she and Mom were locked in a battle of wills about Phoebe borrowing her car for the weekend to visit friends in Quogue, out on Long Island. Mom didn't want Phoebe to have it, but Dad had already promised. (Why didn't I paint *my* name on the bedroom wall? She has that man trained.) So, in between Mom's beatific stares across the sea at the statue, she and Phoebe were picking at each other. And the drama behind the drama was that Phoebe, still working as a hostess while her foot was healing, was still waiting to be ratified by her union to become a member, but was now thinking that maybe she'd rather work at a fashion magazine instead. Though she made no effort to job hunt. And while all this was going on, Mom was helping support her, and, big surprise, Phoebe was running up major credit card debts. Her latest necessity was earrings, charged to Mom. (The grown-up version of standing on the desk and yelling.)

Even though the two of them were having problems, my relationship with Phoebe had definitely improved since she had broken her foot. We spent more time together without Mom, which let us be people more, sisters less.

The ferry moved slowly. "Let's just swim," Phoebe suggested. "It'll probably be quicker."

Mom walked away from her, closer to the railing, so she wouldn't miss a thing.

"Why don't you have a better attitude about this?" I asked Phoebe. "It's a big thing, the Statue of Liberty. You know, 'Give me your huddled masses, yearning to be free.'"

She looked at me blankly. "Whatever," she said.

I went over to Mom, who was absorbed in her moment. And guess who came over to join us, once she was left sitting by herself with no audience for her wisecracks. She looked over at Ellis Island.

"I guess that must have been sort of moving to see when you came from your wretched town in Europe," Phoebe said, to no response. "Wait on line, have your name changed, your identity stolen. Did they see the Twin Towers when they got here too?"

Mom sighed. Mightily.

It was the same between them as always. Neither would confront the other directly. Just needle. Or ignore. Subterfuge and counterattack.

"I want to go to the top of the flame," Phoebe said, knowing full well she couldn't. I glared at her. Enough already.

I tried resurrecting our spirit of adventure.

"Mom, tell me again what happened when you went with your family to the Lincoln Memorial," I said. "I forget how it goes."

"Well," she said, in a tone that after all these years still brimmed with grudge, "We had gone to Washington and we were supposed to see the Lincoln Memorial, but I was wearing a coat that had a rip in the sleeve because it was toward the end of the season and I needed another one anyway, but Grandma said to just wear it on this trip. And then she decided that we couldn't go to the Lincoln Memorial after all because my coat was ripped. And I was devastated by that because I had really looked forward to it, you know?" Her face looked about eight years old, fresh with disappointment and that helpless fear of childhood when things around you happen too fast to ever control them. "And Grandma kept saying, 'We can't go because your coat is ripped' and finally I didn't know what else to say, so I told her, 'Lincoln won't mind.' So we went."

Oh, Mom. I put my arm around her shoulders and headed off the boat.

The statue was enormous. As we got closer we saw we had two options. We could either walk 354 steps to the crown, or take the elevator to the pedestal.

Now, here was a conundrum. First, we had Mom, the field trip queen, making up for lost time, facing 354 steps. And though she was practically turning green at the thought of climbing them, she said, "Sure, I'll do it." Then there was Phoebe, recently off her crutches and making good use of both feet by shifting from one to the other, somehow thinking that even though her friends wouldn't be ready to go to Quogue until 5:30 and it was now all of 10:00, if we hurried she could get there sooner. I looked back at the sign, which also said that because of the crowds all trying to climb to the top of the stairs at once, the entire process could take between two and three hours.

"What if you're halfway up the stairs and feel that you want to go down again?" Phoebe asked.

"Well, then you're stuck," I said. "You either do it or you don't."

My own feeling about this was, who were we kidding? Mom taking on 354 stairs was something I knew she was crazy enough to do, whether or not she ever walked again. She would grin and bear it all the way to the top of that crown and back with a big fat I-told-you-so on her face. If she could plant a flag at the top when she got there, maybe even publish some navigational maps for the journey so that others who ventured forth after her could find their way, she'd do that too.

"Maybe we can try to exhibit some mental health here," I offered. "Mom, you know these steps would be hard for you. And they'd be hard for Phoebe with her foot. And even though mine is healed now, I'm just a baby and don't want to do it either."

Mom seemed to soften a little. Like maybe if we didn't have to climb after all, but it wasn't her choice, her fault, then maybe she could live with that. Fine. Despite my considerable efforts toward separating from Mom into a fully formed emotionally mature adult, here I was taking a day off from work to make her fourth-grade dream come true, so why shouldn't I take the blame of wimping out on the climb? Wasn't it enough that we were here? Wasn't the view of Manhattan going to be just as spectacular from the pedestal as it would have been from the crown? And didn't the shitty little fourth-grader picking his nose on the line to climb those stairs deserve to live another day? Which he certainly wasn't going to do if I had to stand next to him for three hours.

Phoebe settled it after looking at the crowd squeezing through the door. "Two to three hours with all those people crammed on the stairs? Forget it. I'd freak. I just don't have the patience for it. I guess if you're ten, it's sort of cool," she said dismissively.

That was enough for Mom. "It's the kind of thing that sounds like a great idea when you're not here," she said agreeably.

Good. We were not going to be trapped on the stairs for three hours, and we weren't going to get into any fucked-up neurosis about overcoming our limits and persevering despite all odds. We would just get into the elevator and go to the pedestal. And that would be enough. My God, what was the date? Could this family be saved? Could the answer be yes?

Of course not. Three minutes on line for the elevator and Mom started studying the staircase. "We've been in this country too long," she declared, her voice ringing with self-reproach. "The strength of that European stock has been diluted. We should be able to just take the stairs."

I sighed. Was the pedestal high enough to jump from?

Now she was onto the flame. "It's not how I remember it," she carped, surveying a current picture. "It was bigger, more prominent." Okay. It was the flame's fault that we were on line for the elevator.

Finally, we were on our way up. Then we had to walk a few flights to the pedestal. Now that we'd actually climbed some steps, there were no more complaints about stock and stamina. Twenty-four suddenly seemed more than enough.

The view was glorious, both of the river and Manhattan. Phoebe leaned over the railing. "I'm gonna spit," she announced. She watched for a moment. "It didn't go all the way down."

"Phoebe that's awful," I said. "There are people down there."

"They'll think it's raining," she said.

Mom was thoroughly disgusted. "Why would you even *think* of spitting?"

"'Cause it's fun to see where it lands," Phoebe said, unperturbed. "Want to watch?"

"I'm not at all interested," Mom said, turning her back.

I sighed. When I'm with Phoebe alone or talking to her on the phone, the dynamic is thoroughly different. More and more, she's a peer. More and more, I let her be. But put Mommy in the mix with me and Phoebe's suddenly hellbent on being a three-year-old.

She spit again, to drive Mom insane. Maybe even drive her insane enough so she would just let Phoebe take the car straight from the city out to the beach instead of having to drive Mom back to Scarsdale first. Which was the torture she had worked out to punish Phoebe. That must have been some pair of earrings. Or maybe she had been pushed too far when Phoebe suggested that since she had really been working so hard for so long without a break, she might take a vacation in Jamaica with friends. And how would she pay for it, Mom asked. You guessed it. Credit card.

So, Phoebe knew exactly why Mom was pissed off, maybe even that she deserved to be. That was why she was spitting, committing an act that was not only rude but highly unsanitary. Because with her lifelong phobia of runaway germs, nothing drives Mom crazier than unsanitary. "Don't eat from the community pot!" she'll yell whenever we taste her chili or spaghetti sauce or whatever is in there with a spoon and then go to dip it back in.

I tried to ignore them both. The day was not sunny, but the water gave off a glare and I had to squint against it to look up at the statue. I could see only a small segment of it. And it occurred to me, after all the effort expended in getting us there, that the damn thing was best appreciated from a distance. Just like my family. Like anybody's family. When you get too close the promise of a divine haven evaporates somehow, and all you've got left is a bird's-eye view of a gigantic copper foot in a sandal while your twenty-eight-year-old sister is spitting to upset your mother, who, after all these years, still doesn't want her to borrow the car, while for once, you're being left mercifully out of it.

I had been right, after all, at the age of five, to want to be Peter Pan. I was apparently never going to grow up anyway. The least I could have gotten out of it was being able to fly. Anywhere.

Mom headed away from Phoebe and smiled at me. "Finally, I've achieved closure," she said, greatly pleased.

Well, that's one of us.

We found a bookstall inside with various histories of the statue's construction. I learned two things. First, that the poem about the Statue of Liberty was written by Emma Lazarus, not Emma Goldman. I don't know how I had gotten the notion that it was Emma Goldman, because if you give the idea half a second of real thought, it doesn't make any sense. Second, it's not huddled masses yearning to be free, but yearning to *breathe* free.

I rushed to tell Phoebe, convinced I'd taught her something wrong that she would remember to the end of her days.

"It's *breathe* free, not *be* free," I said.

She yawned. "Whatever."

We entered the exhibit describing the statue's construction. Phoebe rushed ahead, diving into one of the Whitman's Samplers I had found in Washington and brought for her and Mom as field-trip presents. Mom always used to buy them for us and put the little yellow boxes on our pillows as a surprise. We would unwrap the cellophane and run our fingers over the logo on top, which looked embroidered like an old-fashioned sampler, and then open the box and take out the stiff white paper over the four chocolates inside. Sometimes there was a diagram that told you which was which. I would save the caramel, my favorite, for last.

That box innovation was short-lived, it seemed. Phoebe came back. "What do you think this one is?" she asked, holding up a piece covered in dark chocolate. She was really irritating me now. My bright future with her as my peer was looking dim.

"I have no idea, Phoebe. Just try it," I said impatiently. She took a bite and spit it back into the box.

"Coconut!" she shrieked. "Gross!"

I turned away, trying to concentrate on the history of Bartholdi, the sculptor who designed the statue. As I went on I noticed that Mom was still far behind me, reading every single word she could find. And while I saw Phoebe already at the end rolling her eyes because she thought Mom was doing this solely to spite her, I knew better. Mom was doing this because she couldn't climb to the top. She was going to learn every detail and commit it to memory everlasting because that was what she could do.

One segment of the exhibit in particular caught my eye. A placard read: "Beneath the serene and classical features of Bartholdi's Liberty some have recognized the stoic face of his mother, a similarity that the sculptor himself suggested. Although people have offered both patriotic and psychological explanations for this unusual resemblance, Bartholdi's motives remain a mystery."

Some mystery. This was news, that people are haunted by their mothers? After writing up the interview for the *Times* that Mom and I did with William Shatner, I received a letter I found truly funny. It was from a man, a shrink of some sort, from Pennsylvania, I think, who commended me for bringing my mother on this assignment. The only detail he had wrong was that he thought I was a man too. "Most men bring their mothers with them wherever they go, but only in spirit," he had opined. "How refreshing and brave of you to do so in the flesh. Has it ever been done before?"

Of course I was tempted to write back, to expound on the perils of projection and its many ramifications on the spirit and the flesh, but I restrained myself. He might be the type to be so embarrassed he'd go home and shoot his mother. In the flesh. And then it would be my fault.

I caught up with Phoebe, who was pacing near the exit. Along with photographs, there were quotes displayed from people who had immigrated and recalled their first impressions upon seeing the statue. One said: "She held such promise for us all with her arm flung high, the torch lighting the way. Opening a new world to those who would accept the challenge."

Phoebe read it with me. "You know what freaks me out about this?" she asked. "Look at the faces. Even though they're coming from a terrible place to a better one, they're still so scared. None of them knows what's going to happen next."

Mom approached. She was crying. "It's really touching," she said.

"It really is. We don't understand the meaning of freedom here. We're so used to it."

We kept on looking. I thought about what Phoebe said, that no one ever knows what will happen next. To me, that is the hardest part of life. I know it's supposed to be one of the best parts, that element of surprise, when wonderful fabulous things can happen suddenly and make you joyful about being alive.

But how many of those moments are there, compared to the bad? To the dangerous or downright destructive? The day someone runs a silly errand, like picking up a Social Security card in a Federal building, and never comes home? Or the day a mother takes her three-year-old daughter swimming in a municipal pool and changes her life forever? It's the randomness that's so terrifying. The complete and utter lack of control we all have while we are scheming and planning as hard as we can, desperate to pretend otherwise.

The people in these pictures came because they wanted a better life. Not perfect. You can see that by their faces. Just better. Better than dirt-poor. Better than starved. It's really all anyone can hope for, to wake up in the morning and find better. Whatever the stakes are—as big as a blood test or as small as an invitation. Each day promising a chance for relief, even celebration, a sign that good does offset bad. A chance. And that we will be there to see it.

I looked at the dates on the wall for Emma Lazarus, the poet. Born in New York City in July 1849. Died in New York City in November 1887. Thirty-eight years old. Why? Of what? Did she leave children behind? A husband who remarried? Were her parents heartbroken? Was she alone in a garret, shunned by all who knew her because she didn't have children, but wanted to write instead?

I decided I didn't want to know. What I wanted most, actually, was to go home.

We walked back outside and by now, around noon, the line to

climb the stairs was huge, snaking far, far back. Phoebe was practically prancing with impatience.

"Let's get out of here," she said, racing toward the ferry.

"I want to sit down," Mom said. I could see she was tired. So was I. And it wasn't just physical. There was something about this place that really took it out of you. Maybe it was the responsibility of freedom. The feeling that now that you have it, now that all your relatives earned it for you, exactly what are you doing with it?

"I have to pack for Quogue," Phoebe started, looking longingly at the boat.

"I don't think she should be allowed to control this day," Mom said, half under her breath.

"What did she say?" Phoebe demanded. Not of Mom, mind you. Me.

"She said she doesn't think you should be allowed to control this day. And neither do I. If you want to go back now, go."

Well, then she looked lost. First of all there was that fancy lunch we had planned. Second of all, if she let Mom out of her sight now, she knew it was good-bye car, period.

"Mommy wants to sit down and that's what we're doing." I set off toward a pretty plaza filled with wrought-iron tables and chairs. The two of them followed.

Mom and I smoked and attempted to chat. Phoebe, sensing herself perilously close to complete ostracism, chimed in too, all sweetness and light. Mom started talking about the fifty-four-year-old bologna sandwich. And suddenly, sitting out there in the cool, damp air, I was ravenous. That bologna was sounding better than any risotto ever could. I remembered that when I was very small, Mom used to have a butcher who would give me a slice of it whenever we went there. It was our best errand.

Phoebe started saying *yum*. She was trying to make amends, jumping on the bologna bandwagon, posthaste.

"Should we just ditch Gotham and go back to my house and make bologna sandwiches?" I asked. "We could even use white bread."

This prompted a unanimous chorus of *mmmmmm*'s.

"Are you sure you want to?" I asked Phoebe. "I know you had your heart set on Gotham."

"No—for bologna, I'm happy to give it up," she said angelically. Maybe she was, but the fact also remained that it was quicker to eat a sandwich at my house, right around the corner from her apartment, than go to a restaurant downtown.

"Mom?"

She nodded happily. "Absolutely."

I called the restaurant and cancelled, and along with a huge crowd got back on line for the next ferry. When it arrived we practically ran to get seats, settling on a bench with Mom in the middle. We both put our heads on her shoulders to sleep.

Which didn't last long. Two little girls standing next to us were perfecting a complicated version of Miss Mary Mack, an upscale patty-cake.

"That's gotten more sophisticated than I remember it being," Mom said. I nodded. Phoebe didn't stir. When we let passengers off at Ellis Island, the boat rocked in the water awhile.

I looked at the New York City skyline, so glamorous, so safe. Safe because it was mine—my city, my home, the view I had had all my life. The place I had come all my life, with my family. And they would always be my family, even if I did grow up. But what would that mean, exactly, to grow up? To become magically self-contained and have all the answers? Sure. To not need Mom? That would never happen. She used to tell me stories about visiting elderly people in the hospital for one of her gerontology courses and hearing eighty-year-old women in pain, still calling for their mothers.

Maybe growing up meant freedom from my childhood self. That I might finally stop trying to fix the world for Mom, or fix Mom for the world. Or not. Childhood selves die hard, after all. Maybe what it really meant was that when I tried and didn't succeed, I would be able to recognize how much she loved me, anyway. Just for me.

Maybe growing up meant that Phoebe and I would evolve so completely that we'd eventually replace Mom in each other's lives after she was gone. No. We won't. We will be the younger and older sisters we always were, just with the added benefit of time to balance us a little. And we will rely on each other and trust each other because we know we can, and whenever one looks at the other, she will be able to find Mom there still, looking back. Watching.

On the bench, Mom rested her head against Phoebe's, which lay on her shoulder. Their car differences, apparently, went only so far. The boat moved again and I looked toward land, feeling a sudden lift of anticipation. So much lay ahead there. Quogue. Bologna. A better life.

chapter eleven

You'll Never Walk Alone

I t was in second grade, actually, that death first scared me, right in the middle of my Gates Reading Comprehension test. One of the stories that my seven-year-old mind could not comprehend was about an old woman who finished her daily chores, lay down on her bed and decided to die. And did.

The idea of death as free will had never even occurred to me. Did that mean both my grandmothers could make the same decision? Or even worse, could Mom?

We were always told that if Mom and Dad died together, the plan was that we would go live with Aunt Marcia and Uncle Bernie. And with all due respect to their kind hearts, this was not a prospect I remotely welcomed—especially since the weekend we stayed over there and in the middle of our running around the yard whooping it up, Aunt Marcia came outside and told us that we needed to be quieter because she didn't want the neighbors to think her family was loud just because we were Jewish. A prospective life of silence simply did not appeal.

But Dad seemed to take extra measures to ensure that he and Mom would not die together. When the family took airplanes on vacations we would split up. Me, Dad and eventually Emmett on one plane, and Mom, Phoebe and Greg on the other. That way, the reasoning went, if one crashed, the other half of the family would survive. (Of course, the six of us went everywhere in the same car, but let's not get logical about something like death.)

In the beginning, I didn't mind the flying setup at all. The first time we tried it, I was almost eleven and we were going to California. I was very excited about this trip, and I definitely got the best end of the deal. At that point Emmett hadn't been born, and Phoebe was only a little more than a year old. Because of his business, I think, Dad and I flew first-class, while Mom and the other kids flew coach. I ate Oysters Rockefeller. Mom ate Maalox. It seems that the pediatrician had given her some drug to put Phoebe to sleep for the long flight, but Phoebe being Phoebe had a bad reaction to it and became hyper. She screamed for almost six hours. While she did, I watched Terence Stamp in *Blue* and sipped Dad's champagne. By the time we met up with them at the airport, I felt soigné enough for silk stockings. Mom felt ready for a breakdown. On the trip back home, she skipped the medication and Phoebe was a delight, helping all the stewardesses. Or at least that's what I heard. I was too busy eating cioppino to care.

I got mine, though. On Greg's great bar-mitzvah journey to Jerusalem, I flew coach with Dad and Emmett, who was about three years old at the time. The flight was something like sixteen hours and Dad had the notion of laying Emmett down on the seats while I slept on the floor, so that if he fell, he would fall on me. Thankfully, the kid had exceptional balance. He didn't.

So, anyway, the air-travel scheme worked. We all lived. My grand-mothers, unfortunately, did not.

I was nine when Dad's mother, Nana, died. She and I had a mutual admiration society. When she made chopped liver she let me turn the hand grinder, which no doubt made the process three times as long, but she never seemed to mind. When it was finally finished and served in the green glass bowl, everyone said it was a masterpiece and she fostered my delu-sion that it was all because of me. She also never made me taste anything that looked scary, like her lentil soup with dumplings, which I thought resembled mud. Or schav, which was a nasty-looking grassy soup she kept in a jar in the refrigerator. Instead, she made me bologna sandwiches for breakfast, on challah (white bread is made with milk and wouldn't be ko-sher), and giant meatballs for dinner with rice, not spaghetti. She drank her tea from a glass with a sugar cube in her mouth, and to keep her com-pany, I put a Tootsie Roll in my mouth and drank a glass of milk.

She and Mom got along incredibly well, but every once in a while there was a rift in some basic ideology. I usually liked these moments of dissension because it meant that when I was mad at Mommy, I could find solace at Nana's.

One morning I was in Nana's kitchen playing with an assortment of pots and pans. After clanging them around awhile (there's that noisy-Jewish-girl problem again) Mom held up a pot and said to me, "Is this empty or full?" And, being everyone's favorite firstborn child and grandchild, I sang out with self-congratulatory enthusiasm, "Emp-ty!" Nana nodded proudly, while Mom shook her head. "No," she said, "it's not. It is full of air."

Well, judging from Nana's expression, she felt the same way about physics and molecules that I eventually did. As far as she was con-cerned, that pot was empty. End of story. While Mom beamed over her Science 101 tutorial, Nana said nothing, but I knew that she was might-ily displeased by this misrepresentation of the facts.

The only other time I saw Nana register disapproval of Mom was at the dinner table with me and Kiki, who is Dad and Marcia's older sister. Assuming that I wasn't paying attention, Kiki and Nana were discussing a conversation I had had with Mom in which I told her I was worried about her dying. "Don't be silly," she had reassured me. "I'm too busy to die." Kiki repeated this last bit of dialogue and Nana shook her head at its glibness. Then I think, though I can't be sure because she realized at just that moment that I was actually paying acute attention after all, she said "Meshugge," but caught it before it came out too loudly.

I was upset by this. If my mother told me she was too busy to die, that meant she was too busy to die. She told the truth, as she had taught me to. I had accepted her answer, but suddenly, with a mouthful of meatball, I saw that I had been taken for a fool. Being busy might not stave off death, after all. Nana seemed convinced of that. Now what?

I didn't know it then, but Nana had had leukemia for quite some time, and no matter how busy she kept making chopped liver and stuffed cabbage, she knew she was going to die. She was buried on Dad's birthday, actually. And since I had been pretty well shielded from the last stages of her illness I had somehow gotten the notion that between it being Daddy's birthday and Mommy saying that so many people would come to the house to visit, we were going to have a party called shiva. I proposed that I wear my pink chiffon dress-up dress with the round white collar. Mom gently tried to explain that this was not a festive occasion, which surprised me. I had just assumed that Nana would be at her own funeral. The fact that she was really gone hadn't occurred to me.

I ended up wearing a lavender dress with my white lace stockings and black patent leather Mary Janes, and was absolutely astonished by the experience, beginning to end. It seemed inconceivable to me that anyone was *in* the coffin at the front of the funeral chapel, much less

Nana. Then, at the cemetery, Kiki laid her head on Dad's shoulder and sobbed, in total surrender, it seemed. I couldn't place her, suddenly. She was someone who usually laughed a lot and wore red lipstick and painted my fingernails. We were pals. And she didn't even seem to notice I was there.

Back at the house, there were bagels and lox and, indeed, lots of people, but as parties went, there was something about this one that was definitely off. The mirrors were all covered up with towels (when you're in mourning you're not supposed to be vain, so it doesn't matter how you look), and torn black ribbons were pinned to sleeves. The quality of the laughter was different too, muted somehow. Aunt Marcia burst out laughing at something someone said and then immediately started to cry. Very confusing.

And for months afterward it seemed that Dad was always in a bad mood and Mom would say it was because he missed Nana. But we didn't mention anything because she told us he didn't like to talk about it. He got up early every day though, and before he went to work went to temple to say Kaddish for her. Every single day for a year. I used to think that was so awful, such a dreadful imposition of time and energy, but I can see now how it keeps a connection, a real live duty, which at the very least fosters the feeling that the person is there, still a part of your life. For just a little longer, anyway.

In the meantime, Grandma was doing just fine. She married again, a nice enough man named David, though truth be told I never liked him much. Being thirteen at the time, I didn't like anyone much. "Who *is* this guy?" I asked Mom, whose only answer was "He's a nice man and Grandma likes him, that's who he is." Grandma said she liked his feet. She said they were very small and clean. I guess to her that meant a lot. She had never gotten past her fixation on her feet, which in later years was amplified by an impressive assortment of bunions and corns. On the trip to Jerusalem, when she was scheduled to go to the Mosque of Omar, she decided at the last minute that she couldn't because she would have to remove her shoes to go inside.

"Everyone will see my feet," she fretted to Mom, who looked at her, baffled.

"You would miss one of the greatest sights of the Middle East because you think everyone else is there to look at your feet?"

She was right, of course, but Grandma wouldn't budge. She never saw the mosque. And she liked this man for his feet. In her world, it made perfect sense.

He died when I was a junior in high school. Grandma was upset, of course. I remember that after his funeral I made her a sandwich, cream cheese and dietetic jelly, and it was the first time all day that she smiled and had some color in her face. But she never spoke about him the way she had about my grandfather, who died when I was three. After that, she worked for a while as a nurse in an eye doctor's office. And she used to tell me that she would sit at her desk sometimes and imagine that if she looked up, she would see Grandpa peeking around the corner saying *hi*, the way he used to when he came home from work. She would shake her head then and wipe her eyes and mumble something that sounded like "Mama." It made her sad.

During my last year in graduate school, Grandma started acting funny. Always immaculate, she would come over wearing a blouse with a stain on it. Mustard, maybe, or some food. And I would point it out to her because she always chided me for slumping and not having good posture, so I was glad to return the favor. But instead of jumping up and going into the kitchen for club soda and salt to take the stain out she would just frown at it in a sort of abstract way and shrug. Then she started calling Mommy at six in the morning and then again four more times before seven. The doctor later said she was having small strokes, which made her forget she had called the first time. And there were complications from her diabetes too, which also affected her memory.

The year before she died, she forgot my birthday for the first time ever. Mom was incredibly upset by that. Every time she talked about it, her tight mouth appeared.

Then Grandma started going to the hospital. She had lost her hair, but she wore a wig that mimicked the style of her jet black hairdo, which in later years was accented by perfect streaks of white. When I went to visit her once, she didn't seem to realize that people were there and took the wig off. Which was even scarier than it had ever been seeing Nana without her teeth.

After Grandma got out of the hospital I went up to Spring Valley, New York, where she lived and took her to lunch at a deli in the shopping center near her house. As we got out of the car to walk across the parking lot she wrapped her arm around my waist and smiled close into my face. "You're a nice person," she said approvingly. "You have a good feeling about you."

I hugged her back and after lunch we stopped in at a boutique where she liked to shop. She found a navy-and-white polka-dotted blouse that she took into the dressing room to try on while I waited out front.

"Boy, does she look terrible," the saleswoman said. "I heard she was sick but I haven't seen her in a while. I don't think she's going to make it."

Well, I didn't know how to react to that. Or who she thought she was saying it to. I guess she figured I was one of those companions you see older women walking around with hired for the job when no one else wants to do it for free.

I think I actually said nothing, which was a record of sorts, but I really had no words. I was twenty-four years old and no closer to understanding death than I had been during that second-grade test. Grandma was Grandma, Mommy's mother, in my life always. She made great spaghetti and meatballs. She sewed patches on our jeans and mended hems while she watched her "story" on TV—*As the World*

Turns. She was aces with a crossword puzzle and had the world's greatest taste. And she was cool. When she took care of us during a vacation when Mom and Dad went away, I was fifteen and had some vodka at a friend's house. Grandma took one look at me and said, "Why are you so cocky-doodled?" I had to laugh. It was the perfect word.

She came out of the dressing room and said she had decided that even though the blouse had short sleeves, which would expose her heavy arms, she would buy it anyway because she could wear a long-sleeved white top underneath. I agreed. It was beautiful, I told her. She wrote a check for $22 in her spidery handwriting, while I prayed that the saleswoman wouldn't say anything awful. And I took her home.

That was in June. Over the summer I lived at home and worked in the city, mostly at night, managing a theater, so I didn't see her. She would call constantly, sometimes crying, sometimes not. She wanted things. She called Mom and told her she didn't have enough food. She said she needed Swiss cheese and she had no one to take her to the supermarket. She actually lived in a complex with other senior citizens and there were plenty of people to take her, but somehow she couldn't arrange her schedule for when they wanted to go. So, Mom left her class, left something on the stove at home for dinner and drove the forty-five minutes to Grandma's to take her shopping. When they got back to her apartment, Mom went inside to help her put away the groceries. And found four packages of Swiss cheese in the refrigerator.

In October, Grandma went into the hospital for the last time. One night I got home from work about midnight and saw that all the lights in the house were on. I walked in and Mom was sitting on the living-room floor, sorting through trays and serving bowls. "Grandma died," she said. "I have to set up for shiva."

I dropped my keys and went to her, hugging her, telling her how sorry I was. She seemed stoic about it. She said that she and her two brothers had been with Grandma earlier in the afternoon. That she had asked Mom about each one of us individually, as if to reassure herself, Mom said, that we were all right and she could go. The three of them went out for a cup of coffee, and when they came back she was gone. Mom insisted on seeing her anyway, and she said it helped her. She said she was really gone, that she had no sense of the person being there anymore.

Mom, of course, did not get up early and go to temple every day for a year to say Kaddish. It wasn't her way. She did the reverse. She stayed up late and couldn't sleep. She watched old movies until 4:00 A.M. She cried at almost anything, a commercial or the weather report. She had an enormous amount of unresolved junk with that woman, and her only choice was to resolve it alone, a choice she clearly did not want to make.

Because it wouldn't be nearly as satisfying to work it out now. Without Grandma there, how could Mom strive for redemption? How could she ever make it up to her that even though she was born perfect, she hadn't stayed perfect? Her chances were over. Her Mommy Mirror had disappeared and the last reflection she had seen was frozen forever. It didn't seem to matter that her behavior had been nothing short of perfection. That she had taken every call, no matter the hour or the frequency, made every visit, talked to every doctor. Treated her mother always with the utmost respect and consideration. Which is more than I could say for myself. When Grandma would call, literally fifteen times in twenty minutes, I would lose my patience. I would yell. I would say, "Why do you keep calling? What is it that you need?" And she would cry. Because she had no idea why she was calling either.

I felt horrible afterward, of course. But she scared me. I didn't know who she was anymore and I wanted my real grandma back. I'm sure she did too.

Mom comforted me. She kept telling me that it was okay that I had yelled. That Grandma didn't remember that part, just the good parts, the parts when I was a nice person and she had a good feeling about me.

I thought that was very generous of her to say, whether or not it was true. Her relationship with Grandma now had a beginning, a middle and an end, and all she had was time to look back at it and figure out which stage was which, what she could have done, should have done differently to have finally won this woman's undying love and affection. It was useless to tell her that the answer was *nothing*.

One day she was in the kitchen and fell, slamming her elbow so hard I had to take her to the emergency room. It wasn't broken, just banged up. Then she started to lose her hair, in one big patch. The dermatologist asked if someone had died, if it was a time of stress. He said it would grow back. It did.

Gradually, in her conversation, I noticed more talk about dying, with a renewed vigor about living wills and unplugging respirators and don't-you-dare-keep-me-around comments. Let me go, she kept saying.

Now, for a child, no matter what the biological age, this is not the type of topic that warms the heart. "No," I told her. "I can't do that and I'm not going to promise." Neither would Phoebe. So she called Greg, who promptly called me. "I seem to have been appointed the family executioner," he said. "Mommy told me I have to pull the plug."

It was smart of her, actually. While neither Phoebe nor I would have the guts to do it, Greg wouldn't have the guts to see her suffer. He would keep his promise.

With that detail tidily accounted for, I found myself having conversations with her designed to reassure me that she would always be there, in spirit if not body. She would always be watching, she would always be loving me. Granted, much of this followed the very sudden death of Frank's mother, but I found these conversations alternately comforting and terrifying. Mostly terrifying.

Then, when she and Dad actually got serious about selling the house, she took Phoebe and me on a particularly gruesome tour to chronicle who wanted which tchotchke. Her mother had done the same thing with her.

It turned out that I wanted almost nothing, while—I don't have to tell you—Phoebe wanted everything. Then we got upstairs to Mom's jewelry. She was still keeping some of it in the egg carton I had painted yellow in arts and crafts, and the rest in a cigar box I had covered with blue-and-white wallpaper. She never had an enormous amount of good jewelry, but I always liked her pearls. And the pearl-and-diamond earrings I had borrowed for my wedding. And a diamond band that Grandma had left her. Phoebe wanted all those things and everything else too, real or paste.

"Fine," I said about her taking the diamond necklace. "If I can borrow it when I want to."

"Well, maybe. Okay," she said grudgingly.

Mom eyeballed her. "I'm going to look down and know exactly what's going on here," she said in her best schoolteacher tone.

"*Okay,* I said I would," Phoebe said, greatly aggrieved.

Once the move was over, these lists of entitlements were put away, and I might say, at least by me, promptly forgotten. Mom and I had our lunch with William Shatner, we saw the Statue of Libery and then we arranged to rendezvous with Phoebe the Sunday before Thanksgiving to see *Carousel* and spend a night at the St. Regis Hotel. With all *three* of us sleeping there. I had finally gotten over myself. We would kick off the holiday season in style, courtesy of *Gourmet* magazine, for which I was writing a piece.

I was curious, actually, to see Mom's reaction to the show. She had always liked the song "You'll Never Walk Alone." When she was younger and worked in a doctor's office during the summer, she met a guy her age who had also had polio and walked with crutches. He dubbed this song "the polio song," which had jarred her. She had always thought of it as greatly inspiring, and he could only view it as a sour joke.

I had already seen this particular production of *Carousel* but I still cried when Billy Bigelow came back from the dead to help his daughter. Phoebe cried too. Mom did not. She seemed to have a hardness about the show, as if she were pushing at the stage from her seat. At the end, when I threw away my soggy tissue, she slipped her dry one back into her purse.

We went to San Domenico for dinner, an Italian restaurant on Central Park South, where I love the food and wanted them to love it too. We ordered wine and looked at the menu and Phoebe, who had spent her year in Italy mostly in Florence, got right into the swing and ordered a feast, a huge raviolo filled with ricotta, egg and truffle butter. I ordered duck liver ravioli, calories be damned.

Mom scowled. Dairy would bother her stomach, she said. So would meat. She couldn't have anything that was listed. She wanted plain pasta with tomato and basil. I just looked at her. She was going out of her way not to enjoy this day. Not the show, not the dinner. I knew she was still feeling unsettled about the apartment, even though she had made enormous progress there. It had already become unrecognizable as the place she and Dad first moved in to. But maybe she had struck some deal with herself: that until it was exactly to her liking, she wasn't going to let herself relax.

Phoebe looked at me during Mom's recital of woe and rolled her eyes. I rolled mine back. I was going to kick her under the table for good measure, but I couldn't remember which foot was the bad one.

We went to the St. Regis. Our room was very quiet, very plush. And for two. We agreed that someone would hide in the bathroom if anyone came to the door, like Jeanette, the slim woman with the vest and the French accent who told us in the hallway that she was our butler. She looked more like a spy to me. I could imagine her hovering near the door, counting voices.

"I can't believe it," Mom said, riffling through her bag. "I forgot my toothpaste."

Well, this clinched it. Something was absolutely, definitely wrong. "You *forgot* something?" I was panicking. Was this like the mustard stains on Grandma's blouse? My mother, the human Swiss Army knife, capable in every situation known to man, forgetting the most basic thing? And the worst part was she didn't seem bothered by it. She just looked at me.

"I have toothpaste," I said.

"Good," she answered and sat down.

Okay, fine. I could handle this. I'd gotten used to being Mommy with the kids. "Alex, do you have a tissue?" "Alex, do you have a Band-Aid?" "Alex, do I *have* to take the cough syrup?" But even though I'd always been the mommy to Mommy on a part-time basis, the arrangement had its limits. I was suddenly glimpsing the terror that looms when that layer of Mommy that has stood between you and the outside world disappears and the protection is gone. *You* are the adult. *You* are the wisdom. Whatever comes out of your head is the rule, and my God, what if it's wrong?

I was starting to hyperventilate. Couldn't she have just packed the fucking toothpaste?

Phoebe was perusing the list of hotel services. "Hey, you can get a glass of milk here for $8.50," she said.

Mom opened a magazine, oblivious. Silence reigned.

I looked around for diversion. And found it.

"Look at this!" There, underneath an end table, was an honest-to-God crystal ball on a small gold stand. "I can't believe this, look! Let's have a séance or something."

Mom shook her head. I ignored her.

"Who do you want to talk to?" I asked Phoebe.

"Grandma," she said, without hesitation.

I waved my hands over the ball. "Calling Grandma," I said a few

times. Mom turned the pages of her magazine. "Grandma, Grandma."
I was intent on irritating her now.

"Ah, there she is. She's bowling." I truly have no idea why I said
that. I had never seen her bowl in my entire life. Though I did see her
jump rope once, which was quite enough.

"She's bowling?" Phoebe asked.

"Yeah, she's having fun. You have any questions, Ma?"

She was silent for a moment. "Ask her how my father is," she said,
still leafing through her magazine.

"He's fine, she says."

"What about Grandma Tessie and Uncle Selig?"

"They're fine too. Do you want to tell her anything?"

She considered briefly. "Tell her I'm enjoying her things," she said.
I consulted the ball, then looked at Mom.

"She says give them back," I told her.

"That sounds like Grandma," she said and laughed.

Well, this was turning into a bitter little game. I stopped.

And I stopped trying to change Mom's mood. If she wanted to
hold her breath until she fell over, let her. Maybe this death thing was
brushing just a touch too close for comfort. Maybe the assignation of
her Wedgwood to the next generation of caretakers had made her realize something she didn't want to realize. For all her chatter about letting her go, maybe she didn't want us to. At least not soon. Maybe she
was talking a good game so we would all feel okay when she did go.
"See, this is what I wanted all along. Death is really a part of life. Nothing to be afraid of. Everything's fine." Well, it would seem that wasn't
exactly the case. Even she (Heaven forfend!) might have a few fears
that weren't going quietly into the night on cue. On schedule. The way
she liked them to. Or commanded them to. Or tried.

So we talked about the marble-topped desk next to the couch. And
the damask wall coverings. And the fine Egyptian cotton sheets, direct

descendants of those great ancestors back at the Metropolitan Museum of Art. She brushed her teeth with my toothpaste and kissed us both good-night. But before she could leave Phoebe's side, Phoebe grabbed her hand and pointed to a ring from Grandma on her finger. "Mine," she trumpeted, looking at me.

"I know, Phoebe. Everything's yours."

Mom got into bed with me while Phoebe got into the other one. She needed to be alone because of her foot.

"Ha-ha, Mommy's in my bed," I started, but my heart wasn't really in it.

"Shut up," she said, sleepily.

The wake-up call came right on schedule the next morning, immediately followed by a knock on the door from room service. Mom disappeared into the bathroom while the waiter wheeled in a table.

When the coast was clear, Mom emerged. She seemed to be in better spirits this morning. So was Phoebe. Of course, Phoebe has always woken up in good spirits. I find it one of her more endearing qualities, especially since she never inflicts them on those of us less fortunate.

Breakfast was cold. Waffles, eggs, sausage, toast. All cold. The coffee was tepid. Mom chewed dutifully. "Cold toast reminds me of hospitals," she observed, drily. And somehow, for no particular reason, that struck us all funny. And as we started to laugh for the first time in a day, I wanted to reach over and throw my arms around her and say, "I don't care about the Wedgwood, and I don't care about your jewelry, and maybe most of all I don't care about separating from you, because so much of life is about being separate, separated, alone, and why should that be the goal? What about being together? Stay."

But I knew now that she was back in her control mode, she would only look at me in her worldly-wise-mother way and say, "I can't, sweetheart. You know that."

So I poured us more coffee. And laughed.

1. How does marriage alter the dynamic of Alex's "comfort marathons" with her sister, Phoebe, and her mother, Barbara? To
   what extent do Alex's preparations for her wedding betray her
   anxiety about leaving the Girls Only club she and her mother
   and sister have established in their family? How do Barbara and
   Phoebe feel about her impending nuptials?

2. "The green couch in our family is not only a destination, but a
   state of mind." What state of mind does the green couch represent to Alex and her sister, Phoebe, and what does it represent
   to their mother, Barbara? Why does the green couch serve to
   sustain the relationship between these women? To what extent is
   the green couch a familial version of the therapeutic couch used
   in classic psychotherapy?

3. Temperamentally, how are Alex and her younger sister, Phoebe,
   alike, and how do they differ? To what extent does Alex's treat-
   ment of Phoebe seem more maternal than sisterly? What does
   the incident involving Phoebe's foot injury reveal about the true
   nature of their relationship?

4. "And here I was now, desperately trying to separate from Mom,
   trying to become myself whether she liked it or not." What exactly does Alex mean when she writes of separating from her
   mother? In what ways does Alex's connection with her mother

seem overly dependent, and why might that be a concern to her? How does Barbara feel about Alex's need for her approval?

5. How does Barbara Witchel embody her daughter's description of her as "the human Swiss Army knife"? What special qualities does Barbara exhibit in *Girls Only*, and in what ways do they compare or relate to memories you have of your mother? Is Barbara Witchel an extraordinary human being, or just extraordinary in the eyes of her daughter?

6. "When no one is more loathsome than your parents, stepparents can look semi-loathsome by comparison." How would you characterize Alex's relationship with her stepsons, Nat and Simon? How does her affection and devotion for them seem related to her decision not to have biological children of her own?

7. *Girls Only* describes Alex's reportorial encounters with a number of celebrities, including William Shatner and June Havoc. Why would Alex find her mother's flirtation with the man behind the character of Captain Kirk especially fascinating and revealing? What does Havoc's assessment, "Your life is such a pillow," enable Alex to understand about the importance of her family to her?

8. "I looked at the New York City skyline, so glamorous, so safe. Safe because it was mine—my city, my home, the view I had had all my life." To what extent does New York City function as a character of sorts in *Girls Only*? How is Alex Witchel's life and work enmeshed with the actual, physical city of New York? In what respects is *Girls Only* a memoir of New York life that could only have been written prior to the events of 9/11?

9. On page 191, Witchel writes "I was suddenly glimpsing the terror that looms when that layer of Mommy that has stood between you and the outside world disappears and the protection is gone." How does the death of her grandmother serve as a catalyst for Alex to talk with Barbara about her eventual death? Why might Alex and Phoebe feel differently about choosing things of their mother's to inherit, and what does that reveal about their acceptance and comfort with the idea of their mother's death?

10. Of the many humorous moments in *Girls Only,* which did you find especially funny and why? How does Alex's relationship with her mother resonate with you in thinking about your relationship with your mother? Do Alex and Barbara remind you of anyone you know? Why is the mother-daughter-sister connection such a complex one?

A Conversation with Alex Witchel

Q: *What initially spurred your decision to write a memoir of your family life?*

A: It wasn't really a deliberate decision. When I was a culture reporter at the *Times* in the early 1990s, I wrote a series of pieces for the Weekend section about fun things to do in New York City. One of the editors had an idea about staying at hotels—something no New Yorker has reason to do—and my first assignment was to stay at the Stanhope Hotel, which has since disappeared. It was a small, beautiful hotel on the Upper East Side (where, years later, John F. Kennedy Jr. reportedly holed up when fighting with his wife). It was right across the street from the Met, where my mom started taking me in grade school, so we decided to turn the story into an opportunity for a girls' weekend, complete with tea. When the piece ran in the paper, the response was enormous; about half from women who couldn't believe I had a good relationship with my mother and spent time with her voluntarily, the other half from mother-lovers, as I came to call them, who had always treasured their mothers and made a point of including them in their lives.

After the Stanhope article, more assignments followed and we had a blast. Then I got a call from an editor at Random House who thought he saw a book in these stories as long as they featured the same cast of characters (one of the reasons I never took my husband, much to his chagrin!). For the book, the existing pieces from the *Times* had to be edited to omit details like prices. (In 1993, I see that I was amazed to be charged sixteen dollars for two drinks at the Stanhope. In some places in New York now, one drink costs sixteen dollars.) And all the pieces had to be expanded to include the kind of emotional content that would be inappropriate in a newspaper-service piece.

So I guess I never thought I was writing a family memoir, which sounds official to me. It was more an account of running around with my mom and my sister, which was just what I did at that point in my life, and in the midst of that, filling in whatever blanks I could about being a woman in her midthirties with a sister ten years younger and a mother whom I always believed liked me best. (Just kidding, Phoebe!)

Q: *How did your mother and sister feel about their sudden exposure in* Girls Only?

A: My mom loved it, mostly because she was so proud of the fact that I published a book. I think she also appreciated being seen not only as a mother, but as a person. I think my sister could have lived without the entire experience, but was nice enough not to mention it. As I finished writing each chapter, I would read it aloud to both of them and offer the opportunity to make any changes. My mom changed nothing. The only thing Phoebe changed was the color of her skirt in one description. I think I said it was peach and she was horrified at the notion that anyone would think she'd wear peach. I figured if that was my biggest problem, I was in pretty good shape.

Q: *Do you have any recommendations to readers who may be considering writing about their families?*

A: Be careful. What tends to happen is that the real people you're writing about stop being themselves and become characters in your story. In *Girls Only*, Phoebe is much more the butt of my jokes than her own person, which is great for me and not so great for her. In the ten years since the book was published, she's settled into a great job at a major ad agency. She's married, has a three-year-old son, another on the way and works full time. She's grown-up, responsible and much more in the "real world" than I am as a writer who spends most days sitting alone in front of a computer in her nightgown, waiting for dinner.

Q: *At the time you wrote* Girls Only, *you were in the early years of your marriage and still adjusting to your new role as stepmother. To what extent have the "girls" of your book been supplanted in the interim by the "boys" in your life?*

A: The extent has been enormous, as it would be for anyone with children. My husband had joint custody of the boys, which meant meeting them for dinner every Wednesday in their neighborhood, then having them come to our apartment every weekend. At the beginning, they came Saturday mornings and stayed until Sunday afternoons (in New York City, the age of twelve is the unofficial magic moment when kids can start taking cabs by themselves, offering the equivalent relief and joy as the first time they were able to sit and read to themselves and left you out of it!). Then they started coming after school on Fridays and going back Sunday evenings. And if they were seeing a friend in our neighborhood midweek and wanted to come for dinner or sleep over, that was fine too.

So that was one part of the girls being supplanted. Then, after *Girls Only* was published and I learned to write a novel, I continued to work at the *Times*, so my free time all but disappeared. I saw my mom way less than I ever did before. Same with my sister, who now wakes up early on the weekends to go to events starring Elmo, live and in person.

But the bottom line was, if our kids were here, I was here. End of story.

Q: *You have also written a novel,* Me Times Three, *that incorporates some key autobiographical elements. To what extent do you think your attraction to memoir and autobiography is connected to your work as a journalist?*

A: I think I'm always a reporter first. When I was growing up, my mother would sit me down and say, "Tell me about your day." It wasn't enough to say, "I hate math." She expected a full story, replete with detail, about the subjects, the teachers, the kids in my class— what they said, what they wore, how they behaved on and off the playground. I learned to tell her every single thing I could possibly remember and to tell it in a way that kept her interest. Whether I'm writing for the *Times* or creating characters in a novel, it's still all about what I observe and how I tell it at the end of the day.

Q: *How frequently do you and your sister, Phoebe, and your mother, Barbara, manage to see one another these days, and how do you enjoy spending time together?*

A: Far less frequently, as I said earlier. Of course, we see one another on all the holidays. My mom retired from teaching almost three years ago and she's had some health issues, so she and I have spent too much time in doctors' offices for both our tastes. To balance that we try to have lunch together at least once a month.

Q: *In* Girls Only, *you write about your lack of desire for a biological child of your own. What are some of the highs and lows of parenting you've experienced as a stepmother?*

A: One of the highs, interestingly enough, is that my stepkids are thrilled to be their father's only children. In their experience, when their friends' parents divorced, the father usually remarried and had more children, and spent far more unbroken time with his "new" family than his old, so they felt left out. Frank always made the kids his first priority and included them in our lives as much as possible, which was a decision I endorsed wholeheartedly. After all, I never even had to give birth and I got to help raise two interesting, fun, fabulous kids, whom I adore. I thought that was a pretty sweet deal!

Q: *Your husband and stepsons are all writers. Do the four of you talk shop when you're together, and do you act as one anothers' first readers?*

A: I am Frank's first reader and he is mine and that means of everything—both of our pieces at the *Times*, novels, books or freelance articles. I trust his ear and brain and sense of humor implicitly and if something seems off to him, I know he's right. And vice versa.

As for the kids, we both feel it's important to let them find their own voices and they have—in record time, it would seem. Our older son, Nathaniel Rich, published his first book, *San Francisco Noir*, an annotated guidebook to that city through the film noirs that have been shot there, when he was twenty-five. Neither Frank nor I read it until it was finished, and boy, were we impressed! As was Nathaniel's mom, who is a book editor herself and instrumental in making both kids feel empowered as writers. Nathaniel recently sold his first novel and Frank and I were blown away by it.

Our younger son, Simon Rich, published his first book, *Ant Farm*, last spring, while still a senior in college. Simon has been devoted to comedy all his life, it seems. He started a humor magazine in high school and never enjoyed anything more than writing jokes. He's not only truly funny but, like Nat, completely unfull of himself. Also like Nat, Simon didn't show us his book until it was finished. That's a decision that seems to be working well for them both!

As you can imagine, we're wildly proud of them. One friend calls our family "the word factory."

Q: *Were there any anecdotes about your family that you wish you had or hadn't included in* Girls Only? *Can you touch on those briefly?*

A: I can't think of any, really. Looking back on the book now, I can't believe I remembered as much as I did. I do wish I had made a few less jokes, worked a bit harder at fleshing out some emotional issues, but referring back to an earlier question, I think that doing that with family members is very tricky, and no matter how good the intentions, potentially dangerous. So as imperfect as it is—I still wish I could rewrite parts of it—that was my story and I'm sticking to it.

Q: *How often have you fielded requests for your mother's tuna-fish recipe, and do you ever give it out?*

A: Right after the book was published, I was asked for it all the time, and my brothers forbade me from giving it out. (I think that being boys, they were mad about missing all the fun, and this was their only revenge.) I actually gave it to one woman who reviewed the book—she really, really wanted it—and when she saw it she just laughed and laughed because it had so many ingredients. PhD tuna, she called it.

   Since I'm not allowed to share the recipe all I can tell you is this: I have made it myself countless times and it has never once tasted like my mother's. That is not true of her meat loaf or her roast chicken, to pick two other examples, which taste identical to hers when I make them. But as far as the tuna fish goes, the secret ingredient is Mommy. Absolutely no substitutions.

ENHANCE YOUR BOOK CLUB

1. New York City is indivisible from the adventures of Alex Witchel and her sister and mother in *Girls Only*. Would you like to walk in their footsteps with your book club? Plan a real-life or virtual visit to America's most famous metropolis by visiting www.nps .gov/stli to take a virtual tour of the Statue of Liberty, and www .metmuseum.org to wander the galleries of the Metropolitan Museum of Art. If you're planning an actual trip to New York City with your members, check out ww.nycvisit.com for suggestions on where to go and what to see.

2. Were you intrigued by the straight-talking personality of June Havoc, the film and musical star interviewed and idolized by Alex Witchel in *Girls Only*? You may want to hold an in-home screening of some of her films, including *Gentleman's Agreement*, a 1947 film starring Havoc and Gregory Peck, and 1942's *Four Jacks and a Jill*, in which she made her film debut.

3. Barbara Witchel's tuna-fish sandwich represents something of an obsession for her children. What family recipes are you obsessed with? For your book club's meeting, plan to bring along one of your most cherished family recipes. Bring multiple copies of the recipe so that members can trade. You might ask each member of your book club to bring a dish that is especially admired in his or her family, for a special book-club-family-heritage potluck.

Printed in the United States
By Bookmasters